An Official Whitman® Guidebook

Collecting Coins in Retirement

An Action Guide and Estate Advice for Hobbyists and Their Families

With Guidance On Managing An Inherited Collection

Tom Bilotta
foreword by Bill Fivaz

Whitman
Publishing, LLC
PUBLISHING SINCE 1934

Collecting Coins in Retirement

An Action Guide and Estate Advice
for Hobbyists and Their Families

© 2016 Whitman Publishing, LLC

3101 Clairmont Road, Suite G, Atlanta GA 30329

ISBN: 0794843778

Printed in China

Correspondence concerning this book may be directed to Whitman Publishing at the address above, attn: Retirement.

About the Cover: Ray Williams, a colonial coin expert from Trenton, N.J., won third place in Whitman Publishing's "Share Your Hobby" photo contest with this image. The photo, taken by Ray's wife Diane, shows Ray studying his collection at his desk. Appreciating one's coins in such a manner, carefully weighing their emotional value versus the potential returns of their sale, and considering their significance as family heirlooms are all important tasks to undertake in retirement.

This book is designed to provide accurate and authoritative information with regard to the subject matters covered. It is distributed with the understanding that Whitman Publishing and the author are not engaged in rendering legal, financial, or other professional services. If financial or tax advice or other expert professional assistance is required, the services of a competent professional should be sought. The guidance herein is subject to differences of opinion. Before making decisions to buy or sell numismatic collectibles, consult the latest information, including current market conditions. Past performance of the rare-coin market, the bullion market, and commodities markets, or any coin or series within those markets, is not necessarily an indication of future performance, as the future is unknown. Such factors as changing demand, popularity, grading interpretations, strength of the overall market, and national and international economic conditions will continue to be influences.

Windows, Vista, and XP are registered trademarks of Microsoft Corporation. Apple, iPhone, iPad, Safari, and MAC are registered trademarks of Apple Incorporated. eBay is a registered trademark of eBay.

Whitman Publishing is a leader in the antiques and collectibles field. For a catalog of related books, supplies, and storage products, visit Whitman Publishing online at Whitman.com.

Contents

Foreword *by Bill Fivaz* iv

Foreword *by Kenneth Bressett* v

How to Use This Book vii

Introduction 1

Section I: For the Coin Collector 2
    Chapter 1: Why Coin Collecting is Different After Retirement 4
    Chapter 2: Devising a Strategy That Works for You 8
    Chapter 3: Consolidation of Your Collection 16
    Chapter 4: Defining Your Collection Objectives 32
    Chapter 5: For the Coin Collector: Selling Coins 42
    Chapter 6: For the Coin Collector: Knowledge of Importance to Your Family 70
    Chapter 7: For the Coin Collector: Preparing Your Collection for Your Heirs 76
    Chapter 8: For the Coin Collector: Allocation to Your Heirs 80

Section II: For Inheritors 102
    Chapter 9: For the Inheritor: Issues Involved in Managing an Inherited Collection . . . 104
    Chapter 10: For the Inheritor: Important Knowledge You Will Need 114
    Chapter 11: For the Inheritor: Disposing of Your Collection 124
    Chapter 12: For the Inheritor: Selling High-Value Portions of the Collection 128
    Chapter 13: For the Inheritor: Selling Low-Value Portions of the Collection 136

Section III: For Collectors and Inheritors 142
    Chapter 14: Estate and Tax Considerations 144
    Chapter 15: Other Considerations 148
    Chapter 16: Coin Industry Trends 152
    Chapter 17: Selling on eBay for Enjoyment and Profit 160
    Chapter 18: Other Collectibles 172
    Chapter 19: Technology 174

Conclusion 192

Appendix A: Grading Coins: A Primer for Inheritors 193

Appendix B: Coin-Collecting Resources 243

Acknowledgments & About the Author 245

Glossary 246

Index 248

Foreword

Finally! A comprehensive, user-friendly book on how to prepare your collection for disposition after you leave this planet and how your heirs should handle the coins you have enjoyed so much collecting.

As the author states in "How to Read This Book," the information contained herein is not intended to serve as an expert investment or tax-planning guide; rather, it details how coin collecting differs from your pre-retirement years to your retirement considerations. Many important options are discussed, all of which I know you'll find both interesting and valuable in deciding what to do with those coins you've treasured for so many years.

This is a book every numismatist should read and have in his library! All too often the situation arises where a coin collector fails to spend a little time toward the end of his collecting career to put down on paper exactly how he wants his holdings dispersed after passing. This book will clearly and concisely walk you through the various options open to you.

You've spent countless hours assembling and enjoying your favorite coins, learning their history and admiring their beauty, and you want to pass this experience on to the next caretaker. It may be a family member or a new owner who wants to add your coins to his collection.

Heirs are often confused regarding what to do with a collection now in their care, especially if they have little or no interest in the hobby. What should I do with it? Who do I contact? Will I get a fair price when I sell it?

Tom Bilotta's book answers these questions. He has logically divided the book into three basic sections: the first covering subjects both collectors and inheritors will find pertinent.

His step-by-step presentation in each segment is well thought out and presented. Tom offers various situations in which you may find yourself and offers cogent suggestions for each scenario. One of the most important parts of the book is his 11 "Closing Points" on page 95. Be sure to read these!

The bottom line is this: Tom Bilotta's book is a must-read for every numismatist. It emphasizes the important areas of collecting that have really not been that well addressed before this work, and throughout his writings he emphasizes that coin collecting is—as any hobby should be—*fun*!

Bill Fivaz

Atlanta, Georgia

Foreword

Scientists say people who have hobbies are not just filling time; they may also be extending their life span, increasing their energy level, and living a more rewarding life. There is no question about this in my mind. Those who actively participate in some absorbing activity nearly all live longer, happier lives. And it is never too late for anyone to begin enjoying hobby benefits.

This is not to suggest that simply adding a hobby to your daily routine will ensure you live to a ripe old age. Genetics and a healthy lifestyle play a major role in how long we live. We all have the potential to live longer if we do the right things and get a bit lucky. Adding an enjoyable hobby to the mix has been shown to minimize stress and increase creativity. It may also foster a sense of achievement and mental development.

So, will having a hobby help you make it to your 100th birthday? Almost certainly it will help, but other factors are also important. Longevity is largely dictated by healthy habits and genetics passed on to you by parents and grandparents. Make no mistake, however: you can add to your chances by learning how to prepare for that expanded lifespan through practices that you can adopt today. This might be something as obvious as changing old habits like smoking or excessive TV watching, and getting back to golf, outdoor walking, cooking, arts and crafts, or dancing.

Many people who embark on hobby interests late in life do so by returning to something that was of significance to them in their youth. This seems to be particularly true of those who take up music again, or try to be more serious about painting, or decide to add to the stamp or coin collection that was put aside when life became too filled with college, work, and raising a family. While it often feels like we never have enough time to add to our activities, there usually is some available time that can be devoted to anything that is important enough to enrich our life. If you already have a hobby or two that by now is a habit, you can renew your enthusiasm by exploring new interests that will offer new experiences.

Healthy habits slow aging, as do any activities that stimulate spiritual, mental, and social responsiveness. The fact is that attitude plays a crucial role in the way people age. Adults who have a positive attitude about getting old live longer than those with negative thoughts. Salustiano Sanchez, who was the world's oldest man and lived to the impressive age of 112, found pleasure in his gardening, crossword puzzles, and nightly gin-rummy games with friends. His hobbies, whether he knew it or not, endowed him with major health benefits and a long and happy life.

A person can be very old at 50 or very young at 90. It depends on attitude, health, drive, and motivation. Some of the more popular hobbies include reading, exercise, walking, sports, music, collecting, volunteer work, pets, and yoga. The choice is up to you.

And if none of these work, fib about your age. Add five or ten years to your actual age, and people will tell you how fit and young you look.

Kenneth Bressett

Colorado Springs, Colorado

How to Use This Book

If you are a coin collector interested in how to approach collecting during your retirement years, you will want to closely read section I, which covers everything you need to know. Though section II is primarily written for those who inherit collections, and though some of the material duplicates topics covered in section I, it is worthwhile to read section II so that you will gain a better appreciation of the challenges faced by your heirs.

If you are the inheritor of a collection, start with section II, which addresses topics of interest to you in a manner considerate of your situation. Once you have completed section II, it may be worthwhile to browse section I, which will assist you in better understanding the perspective and challenges faced by the collector.

Section III covers topics of interest both to retired collectors and to inheritors.

This book is not intended to serve as an investment guide or expert estate-planning guide; rather, its purpose is to bring to your attention how coin collecting differs during your retirement years from pre-retirement collecting. This should assist you in maximizing your continued enjoyment of the hobby and also enable you to plan for the eventual disposition of your collection. Armed with this information, you will be better able to plan for the sale or allocation of your collection and optimize the results you are able to achieve both for yourself and for your family.

Section I of this book focuses on topics of interest to the coin collector, providing a comprehensive look at the considerations needed to enjoy coin collecting during retirement and also prepare for eventual disposition of your collection.

Chapter 1 discusses those factors that make coin collecting different during retirement.

Chapter 2 aids you in devising a strategy that meets your particular needs.

Chapter 3 describes approaches and reasons to consolidate your collection.

Chapter 4 focuses on your continued collecting pursuits.

Chapter 5 discusses the sale of parts of your collection.

Chapter 6 describes information you will need to provide to your family.

Chapter 7 addresses more specifically planning for your heirs.

Chapter 8 discusses allocation strategies for your estate.

Section II represents a shift of focus to those family members who have inherited a collection and who need guidance on its disposition.

Chapter 9 briefly presents an overview of the considerations facing the inheritor.

Chapter 10 provides some basic information on coin collecting, along with a list of potential resources for those wishing to learn more.

Chapter 11 suggests how to approach the disposition of an inherited collection.

Chapter 12 focuses on specifics regarding the more valuable parts of your collection.

Chapter 13 addresses lower-value components of the collection.

Section III provides coverage of items of interest to both collectors and their family heirs.

Chapter 14 addresses some of the tax and estate issues involved with inheritance and sale of a collection.

Chapter 15 speaks to the non-financial aspects of passing a collection to your heirs.

Chapter 16 describes current coin-industry trends regarding grading, purchase and sale, and protection of coins.

Chapter 17 is focused on the opportunity to use eBay as a sales vehicle for some of your coins.

Chapter 18 discusses how the concepts in this book may be applied outside of coin collecting.

Chapter 19 mentions a few specific technology topics of importance to the coin collector.

Appendix A is a valuable introduction to grading coins by photographs, with a focus on some of the most popularly collected U.S. series.

Appendix B provides some further resources for your numismatic education.

Introduction

Many collectors do not take the time to understand how the parameters of collecting may change during their retirement years, and as a result they experience diminished enjoyment of the hobby and leave their family with a significant burden.

This book is written for two primary readers. The first section focuses on coin collectors nearing or in retirement, who need to consider the best way to pursue their collecting interests and/or prepare their collection for their heirs. The second section is intended for people who inherit a coin collection and need assistance with deciding what to do with it.

The focus of this book is coin collecting, and many of its chapters specifically address the considerations unique to coin collecting. Much of what you will learn here, however, may be applied to any type of collectible.

Prior to retirement, collectors invest a significant amount of time, money, and energy in pursuit of their collecting interests. The typical collector is driven by enjoyment of the hobby and also by a hope that the value of his collection will grow and eventually result in some financial benefit to his family. It is a goal of this book to provide you with detailed information regarding the special considerations of collecting during retirement so that you may continue to enjoy participation in the hobby and also increase the likelihood of realizing the hoped-for financial benefits for your family. A second goal of this book is to assist you in easing the burden a coin collection places on your heirs by encouraging you to prepare a collection for disposition and also providing your heirs with effective strategies for managing their inheritance.

SECTION I

For the Coin Collector

Section I starts by defining the parameters
of coin collecting before and after retirement
and how they differ. It goes on to identify
some collecting strategies intended to maximize
enjoyment and also ultimate financial benefit.

*For many collectors, the parameters of
coin collecting are very different after retirement.*

CHAPTER 1

Why Coin Collecting Is Different After Retirement

The transition from the working world to retirement will bring with it many changes, and these changes may in turn factor into your coin collecting activities.

TIME

Prior to retirement, demands of family and career usually mean that you do not have the amount of time you would like to spend on coin collecting. You pursue collecting activities opportunistically, allowing them to take a back seat to your career and family. You may have begun collecting coins as a child, and as an adult you might find the need to set aside coin collecting for long intervals. Your activity probably occurs during intervals when you have time available, or when ongoing events in the hobby draw your attention.

As you approach retirement, your interest might rekindle. After retirement you find you have much more time available, as family demands and those associated with a career diminish. Now your challenge is to find an approach to coin collecting that will provide enjoyment over your many available hours.

FUNDS

Before retirement, most collectors have more money to spend than after retirement, when income streams are typically lower and funds must be reserved for medical and long-term care.

For those interested in growth in value, the shorter periods of time make it more difficult to view coin acquisitions as likely to provide financial benefit.

With more time but less in the way of monetary resources for acquiring new pieces, the retired collector might continue to enjoy the hobby simply by inspecting and appreciating those coins he's acquired over the years.

◆ ◆ ◆ ◆ ◆

INTEREST

The combination of more time and fewer funds is challenging to the average collector. It may be difficult to define new collecting goals that are attainable. There is also the question of motivation. Many younger collectors believe they are building financial value for the future, whereas older collectors have a more difficult challenge to make this case. Maintaining an interest in the hobby when much more free time is available also results in a need to focus on objectives that provide enjoyment for many more hours.

CONCERN FOR LIQUIDATION

As a young collector you were probably not at all concerned about the possibility of liquidating your collection, and therefore you did not spend time learning about the sale of coins. As a retired collector, you can likely foresee whether someone in your family will be interested in continuing your collection (and financially able to do so), rather than selling it. You are also concerned about equitable treatment of your heirs. You may also need to cash in portions of your collection in order to provide more funding for your retirement.

HEALTH

At retirement age, you are more likely to face health issues that may affect your ability to participate actively in coin collecting. Travel to attend coin shows or to interact with dealers and other coin collectors may be impossible or difficult for you. Fortunately, the Internet can bring much of the enjoyment of coin collecting directly into your home, enabling you to participate despite physical challenges you face.

COMFORT WITH COMPUTERS

As you enter retirement you may be uncomfortable with new technology. While working, you had access to technology assistance via Information Technology or other departments in your workplace. Now, without access to these resources, you must face the challenge of using technology on your own.

The availability of collecting resources accessible through the Internet is too substantial to ignore, therefore it is essential for you to overcome any aversion to using computers. Chapter 19 in section III of this book provides a resource to assist you in approaching technology so that you can overcome this challenge.

Proper consideration of these factors is essential in order to define a collecting strategy that will meet your needs in retirement. These will likely be some combination of continued enjoyment of the hobby, receiving a good return on investment for the purchases made over many years, and consideration of the impact of your collection on your heirs. Time spent to establish a post-retirement collecting strategy will be very productive and will ensure that you optimize your continued role in coin collecting.

* * * * *

Modern technology, especially the Internet, is an incredible resource for coin collectors, and the retired collector could be well served learning about these tools.

*Taking the time to think about how you continue
your collecting activities after retirement is the best way
to assure your continued enjoyment.*

CHAPTER 2

Devising a Strategy
That Works for You

The parameters of coin collecting change in retirement. It is essential for you to understand which of these changes apply in your case and therefore how you will manage your collection.

During your pre-retirement collecting years, most of your enjoyment probably was derived from acquiring coins of interest—and potentially with expectation of growth in value. After retirement your acquisition of coins likely will slow down and might represent a reduced source of enjoyment. You can replace this lost enjoyment with other collecting-related activities.

Two such categories of activities immediately come to mind. First is accepting the challenge of liquidating portions of your collection, seeking to realize maximum value for yourself or your heirs, and also with a goal of reducing any burden you might leave on your heirs. Second is identifying collecting objectives and strategies that are consistent with fewer dollars and more time.

Spend more time on coins in which you have a special interest, and areas where education will help you acquire desirable items. Concentrate your interests, and liquidate portions of your collection that are likely to produce less enjoyment.

The process of selling coins can produce the same level of enjoyment as acquiring them if you sell them wisely and achieve a good return on your many years of investment. Selling coins is a challenge, and one that takes

- time (which you now have),
- thoughtful research,
- willingness to learn, and
- intelligent strategies.

All of these provide the opportunity for continued enjoyment of your hobby.

Focusing your collection on a much narrower set of coins offers you the potential to pursue some very interesting collecting objectives, using available funds and time for in-depth research into topics of interest.

As you refine and focus your collecting efforts, you are also benefiting your heirs by simplifying your holdings.

Your retirement also offers the opportunity for more active participation in coin collecting, assuming your budget, interest, and health allow it. You might choose to share your knowledge and interest with others involved in coin collecting. Such activity can take many forms. If you have in-depth knowledge of some aspect of coin collecting, you might consider contributing an article on the subject to a numismatic publication.

If you are interested in direct contact with other collectors you can join a coin club and participate very actively, perhaps seeking a leadership position.

You might seek to spread interest in coin collecting by speaking publicly at forums attended by potential collectors, especially young people.

CASE STUDY:
NEWLY RETIRED COLLECTOR, RICHARD

Richard recently retired, after having worked continuously from age 16 to 65. During his work life his time was mostly focused on the demands of his career as well as his family, including his spouse of 45 years and three children.

As a young child, Richard became interested in coin collecting. He noticed the variety of designs that appeared in pocket change and sought some basic information at the local library on United States coinage. Armed with this information, he sought to accumulate as many coins as he could from pocket change. This included different types, dates, and mintmarks. At the time, many different designs were still in circulation, including Indian Head and Lincoln Wheat cents; Liberty Head, Buffalo, and Jefferson nickels; Mercury dimes; Standing Liberty quarters; and Liberty Walking and Franklin half dollars.

Over a few years, Richard gathered a variety of coin types, dates, and mints. He purchased coin albums and began to fill them with his finds. He also learned that many coins could be bought in rolls at the bank for face value. He became known to the tellers, who would assist him with his collecting interests.

The coins in Richard's collection were fairly representative of the types in circulation in the first half of the 20th century.

✦ ✦ ✦ ✦ ✦

During his youth, Richard was quite successful at filling his books with most commonly available dates and mints. He also was able to find a few of the key coins for the series he collected, typically in relatively poor condition.

As Richard left his youth, his interest in coin collecting remained, but he needed to focus his time elsewhere. As a young adult, he married at age 20 and needed to focus on supporting his family. He had collected many of the coins that could be found in circulation and did not have funds to acquire missing coins. As a result his activity in the hobby began to wane.

During his adulthood, he maintained awareness of coin collecting, and sometimes significant events would pique his interest and create a spurt of activity. He eventually began purchasing the annual Mint and Proof sets sold directly by the United States Mint to maintain his collection of types and dates. He would occasionally purchase special issues for subjects of high interest.

As he neared retirement, Richard found more time and funds available and began to acquire some coins that were missing from his albums. He learned of many developments that had occurred in the hobby in the years since he began collecting from pocket change.

Many coins had become expensive to purchase and professional certified coin grading had become commonplace. Even if he could afford to purchase one of the coins needed to fill his album, it was not practical to fill the hole as it made most sense for the coin to rest in a certified coin-holder "slab." Richard was happy to be obtaining some of the coins he had been unable to find in his youth, but he never realized the same level of excitement and satisfaction as when he was able to place a newly found coin in one of his albums, in its proper place.

As he raised his family, he had tried to develop an interest in coin collecting in his children, but it never really took hold. Finding uncommon coins in pocket change had become far more difficult and the number of coin designs in circulation had diminished greatly, as modern designs had become locked in for many years.

Richard's wife was very concerned with all of the coins in their house, and had no idea what she would do with them if anything ever happened to him.

After his retirement, Richard found that he had a lot of free time and needed to find some enjoyable and productive ways to utilize it. He had planned well for his retirement needs, but could not afford to spend a lot of money on coin collecting. He wanted to find a way to collect coins without draining his family's assets or creating a large problem for them in the future.

After some consideration, Richard decided that his real enjoyment came from the "thrill of the hunt." That is, he wanted to expend effort to locate coins that interested him rather than just purchasing coins he could afford. During his collecting years, he had developed a strong interest in Mercury dimes and was able to nearly complete an album with specimens ranging from Good to Extremely Fine, with the exception of a few key dates.

Looking through his holdings, he realized that it would not make sense to complete many of the albums that were the core of his initial collecting pursuits. He also noted that some items required a lot of space to store, such as the annual sets he purchased from the U.S. Mint.

Based on his thoughtful analysis, Richard defined a course of action: he would focus his collecting interests on accumulating a complete set of Mercury dimes. He sought to obtain an almost Uncirculated example of every Mercury dime, with natural toning. He chose to seek coins graded AU (About Uncirculated), as this grade encompassed nearly complete preservation of the coin's design without requiring the premium needed to purchase Uncirculated coins. Many Mercury dimes graded AU also avoid

Richard revisited the coins in his albums, selected a few that were significant to him, and earmarked the rest for disposition.

the detracting features, such as dings and bagmarks, often associated with lower-level Uncirculated (e.g., MS-60 or MS-62) coins.

Richard decided that before he would pursue this new collecting objective, he would deal with the remainder of his collection, liquidating as much as possible and marshalling the funds needed to assemble his Mercury dime collection.

Richard went through his coin albums and removed a few coins that were most representative of his youthful collecting activity. He built a small presentation board to display these coins along with a brief history of their significance to him. He then undertook to sell the remainder of his collection. He started by taking a list of his coins to a local dealer, but was disappointed with the offer made.

He spent some time educating himself on the process of selling coins and also on the likely value he could obtain from various portions of his collection. After some self-education and experimentation, over a period of six months, Richard was able to liquidate his collection using a variety of methods. This included auctions, consignment sales, sales in response to the "wanted" ads of mail-order dealers, and finally some sales to the local dealer.

Having freed himself of the weight of his large collection and assembled some funds, Richard began to focus on his new collecting objective. He decided that he wanted to be a very active participant in the process of acquisition. He would be very demanding with respect to the quality of coins he would purchase, seeking the best available specimens with very attractive surfaces. He decided to attend some coin shows so that he could visit many dealers and see many coins to develop an understanding of what was possible.

Based on his initial efforts, Richard was able to identify the key aspects that would render a coin acceptable. He made some initial acquisitions. He also developed a relationship with a few coin dealers who specialized in Mercury dimes and understood what he was seeking and agreed to help.

Periodically he would hear from a dealer who came across one of the coins he was seeking with the attributes he was looking for. Gradually, over a period of several years, Richard was able to obtain most of the coins he sought.

As his Mercury dime collection grew, he sought to expand his activities. He used the Internet to connect with other collectors throughout the country who had similar interests. He also decided to collect some memorabilia relevant to the history of the United States and the U.S. Mint for the period during which Mercury dimes were minted. This period was a very active one in United States history, encompassing both world wars, the Roaring Twenties, and the Great Depression.

Richard managed to fill his retirement years with much activity and assemble a small collection that was very significant to him. This collection was viewed by his family as an heirloom to be kept in the family, rather than a problem to be resolved.

Through his efforts, Richard was able to simplify his collection and remove the burden of disposition from his heirs—and all the while, he was enjoying the hobby he loved.

*Decide what portions of your collection
are really important; then focus your time
and money on those items.*

CHAPTER 3

Consolidation
of Your Collection

If you're a typical coin collector, you may have accumulated thousands of coins over many years of collecting and never taken the time to consolidate your holdings. As a result, the volume of coins has grown to a point of unmanageability even for you as the individual who assembled the collection. If your family inherits such a collection, they will likely be overwhelmed by the daunting task that they face. Families in such situations will often look for a simple solution and sell the entire collection in a single transaction at a fraction of its real value. Your family might also be uncomfortable with the volume of coins and concerned about their safety and the potential for theft.

Part of a typical collection, including some Mint and Proof sets, unsearched rolls and bags, commemoratives, and individual coins.

Holding on to portions of a collection that are not primary to your interest may result in unnecessary annual expenses, such as increased insurance coverage or safety-deposit-box fees. Extra coins also tie up funds that could be used to enhance the core of your collection.

A collection that you have not consolidated can be almost impossible for your heirs to understand. As a result, their efforts to dispose of the collection may realize a poor return on the potential value.

Consolidation represents a major opportunity for you to simplify the challenge your heirs will face. The size of the numismatic holdings are reduced and focused on items core to your collecting interests. It also offers an opportunity to sell unimportant items and use the value generated to enhance your collection, improving your enjoyment and the ultimate benefit that accrues to your heirs.

There are a number of tasks that you should undertake:

- Identify and separate coins that you accumulated (as opposed to selecting with care and study) and that are not of particular collecting interest.
- Identify those coins that are part of your core collection.
- Identify coins with heirloom value.
- Determine portions of your collection you would like kept in the family if possible.
- Equitably allocate to your heirs those coins that will be kept.
- Sell coins identified as not central to your collection.
- Purchase individual coins that will enhance your core collection or enable a more equitable distribution to your heirs.

Only you can assess the value of time spent working with your collection. For those parts of the collection that are not important, should you just place them in a box, drive to a local dealer, and sell them in a single transaction? Or should you invest some time and effort to obtain a higher return?

If you are retired, you might enjoy working with parts of the collection that do not hold much financial value—not concerned by the amount of time you spend as you seek to obtain the best return, understanding that the effort might not be justifiable if a dollar value were placed on your time. Alternately, you might decide that working with such portions of your collection is not a source of enjoyment, and therefore choose to spend your time working with other parts of your collection or activities that represent a better use of your time, either for enjoyment or producing greater financial benefit.

CONSOLIDATION OF YOUR COLLECTION

core collection

new interest

not part of core collecting interest

core collection

BEFORE

AFTER

Large collection containing many items which are not central to your interests

Smaller collection focused on areas of interest along with additional funds to pursue new ones

This sample consolidation reduces the amount of unimportant pieces in the collection; the payoff is the ability to focus on a new collecting interest, as well as additional capital to pursue it.

✦ ✦ ✦ ✦ ✦

You have to decide what is right for you. If you are not enjoying the process and have better uses for your time, don't hesitate to take the easy way out (e.g., quickly selling a portion of coins in a single transaction), doing so with full awareness that it will affect your results.

IDENTIFY AND SEPARATE COINS OF NO PARTICULAR INTEREST

Having a complete inventory of your coin collection is fundamental to deciding how to manage its ultimate disposition. There may be portions of your collection that are not of sufficient value or interest to justify the inventory process. In such cases, the best course of action might be to quickly liquidate these in a bulk sale, not even taking the time to perform a detailed inventory.

Items that are of relatively low value and might be appropriate for a bulk sale include tubes, bags, and boxes of low-grade coins not kept in individual holders. They might also include U.S. government Uncirculated and Proof coin sets, and Uncirculated rolls and bags of recent-issue coins. These items are usually worth cents or a few dollars and cannot justify the effort to catalog them individually. They might not be transacted efficiently *except* in a bulk transaction. Weekly issues of coin newspapers offer buy pricing on such items from a variety of dealers, so it is usually easy to consummate a quick sale with minimal effort and expense.

When approaching the bulk sale of such items, you will want to separate them into several categories:

Government-issued sets in original packaging. These sets are easily identified based on the packaging—often a hard plastic case with a protective envelope sleeve. Typically, inside the packaging there is a small descriptive card detailing the specifications of the coins that are included in the set. This enables you to identify items that may have precious-metal content.

Government-issued Proof and Mint sets are produced in the millions every year and thus rarely become scarce. Such items also have the additional drawback of bulky packaging that takes up additional space.

Government coin sets, as a result of their packaging, often consume far more space than much more valuable individual collector issues. Liquidating these items is a good first step to reducing the bulk. You are likely eliminating items with very low potential for appreciation, and freeing up funds for other purposes. Typically these sets were manufactured in the millions and do not represent a scarce item, or a special part of a collection.

Note that privately assembled Mint sets, and Souvenir sets produced for sale at the Philadelphia or Denver mints or for special occasions, are valued according to the pieces they contain. These items are not listed as sets in standard coin catalogs such as the *Guide Book of United States Coins* (the "Red Book"), and typically are not valued by standard value guides. Care should be taken, as it is often difficult to distinguish third-party sets from official sets due to the fact that the U.S. Mint licenses its logo to some third parties.

Uncirculated rolls of recent issues. This category includes Lincoln Memorial cents, Jefferson nickels, Roosevelt dimes, Washington quarters, Kennedy half dollars, Presidential dollars, Sacagawea and Native American dollars, Eisenhower dollars, and Susan B. Anthony dollars. These coins were minted in large quantities and the rolls are usually valued at a few dollars above face value. Such low-value coins are hard to sell above face value because of the cost of the transaction.

Considering the value of your time, you might find that the best approach is to turn these coins in to the bank for face value. For example, suppose you have 25 rolls of modern dimes with a face value of $125 and a numismatic value of $200. Is it worth one hour of your time and $5 worth of gas or shipping expense (to drive or mail them to a coin dealer) in order to receive an offer of $150? Or would it be more efficient just exchanging them for cash at the bank on your next visit?

It's unlikely to be worth your time to sell rolls of modern issues at their numismatic value when they can simply be spent or turned into a bank.

One exception would be rolls that have never been searched. If you are willing to take the time, you could find scarce die varieties with higher individual values.

Note that in some instances, if rolls of modern coins are included in a sales transaction along with higher-value items, you can eliminate or minimize transportation costs as well as the time you spend, and thereby justify selling such items to a dealer as a part of the larger transaction. One caution, however, is that you need to be careful to assure that you are not actually receiving less value for another part of the transaction in order to appear to be receiving better value for these inexpensive items. Your optimal strategy is to focus on the high-value items and negotiate your best deal for them, and then introduce the low-value items as possible additions to the transaction. In this way, you will know what you are actually receiving in value for each part of the sale.

Boxes, bags, and tubes of low-value coins. This includes such items as low-grade Indian Head and Lincoln Wheat cents, 20th-century nickels, and post-1965 higher-denomination coins. This category does not include coins with significant precious-metal content (all pre-1965 dimes, quarters, and dollars, and pre-1970 half dollars). These coins are usually worth pennies to a few dollars each and are not worth the effort to catalog individually.

A sound approach here is to take the time to sort by date, so that you can identify any individual dates that are key to the series, and therefore potentially of higher value, even at low grade. You can then sell the remaining coins based on the best offer in the "wanted" section of a numismatic newspaper. Most issues of the hobby periodicals contain multiple offers from many dealers, based on coin type (e.g., Indian Head cents, Lincoln Wheat cents, Buffalo nickels, etc.). In some cases a dealer will offer several price points based on approximate grades. In other cases, different prices might be offered based on a date range. For example, Lincoln Wheat cents from 1909 to 1919 are typically more valuable than later dates.

Most likely if you have held these coins for a long time, you have already searched them for the more valuable key dates. In such cases you might be comfortable going directly to liquidation, without searching the coins again. Once again, consider the dollar value of your time. You might not want to spend two hours of time and $20 of mailing and transportation expense to transact 200 coins worth 25 cents each ($50 in total).

Eliminating rolls and bags of coins that you have already searched for key dates is one way of simplifying your collection.

✦ ✦ ✦ ✦ ✦ ✦

Coins with altered surfaces. In recent years, private companies have enhanced the appearance of standard U.S. coins by post-minting altera-tions such as colorizing or gold-plating. Coin series such as the State quar-ters, Territorial quarters, and America the Beautiful ("National Park") quarters lend themselves to colorization. The resulting product may be more attractive or eye-catching than the original coin, but basically these items are classified as "altered" and therefore are unlikely to hold numis-matic value. They are worth only face value, unless for some reason col-lectors are willing to pay a premium. In general you should view such items as not having any intrinsic value; collect them if they provide you with enjoyment, but realize that they are manufactured in large quanti-ties and unlikely to have investment potential.

This colorization was performed by a private party, not the U.S. Mint. It is a coin with an altered surface. Such alteration typically reduces any numismatic value enjoyed by the original coin.

Low-value individual modern coins. These items (which include Eisenhower dollars, Susan B. Anthony dollars, State quarters, and other similar issues) are hard to sell above face value and are most easily disposed of by turning them in at a bank or gifting them to a young collector. You may also want to consider gifting other portions of your collection, such as government sets and low-value collector coins, to benefit the hobby for future generations.

Low-value modern coins might be best disposed of by turning them in at a bank or by gifting them to a younger collector.

* * * * * *

CONCENTRATING ON THE CORE

Eliminating the items above should substantially reduce the volume of your collection, without much effect on the value. Depending on the quantity of such items, you might receive a few hundred to a few thousand dollars, which can be better allocated to purchase a few key coins or used for other family purposes. It is your choice how to best use these funds.

Your efforts along these lines will greatly simplify your collection and reduce it to coins with real value (either numismatic value or precious-metal content). This enables you to focus your remaining attention on these coins, where the value is concentrated.

Once you have eliminated the lower-value and common coins, the next step is to complete an inventory of the remainder of your collection. Depending on the number of items remaining, you might be well served to consider acquiring a software application for managing a collectibles inventory. For smaller collections, a handwritten list, or one entered into a spreadsheet, might be adequate. Some software applications offer the

Inventorying the important parts of your collection that remain will allow you to establish a logical course of action.

✦ ✦ ✦ ✦ ✦

advantage of built-in current market valuations and the ability to print lists of coins for sale, which will aid you during the sales process.

Once you establish a complete inventory, you will want to make an initial separation into three categories:

- ✦ Coins that clearly are part of your core collection
- ✦ Coins that clearly are not important
- ✦ Coins requiring further evaluation

As you make this allocation, do not let the process of selling your coins influence your decisions. The allocation should be based on a simple set of questions. "Is this coin an important part of my collection, or was the means by which I acquired it special?" If the answer is "yes," identify why the coin is important. Does it contribute to the completion of your collection? Do you expect it to grow in value?

If the answer is no, the item should be identified for sale and separated both physically from the core collection and moved to a distinct inventory.

"What if I cannot decide?" Thinking about the reason to keep a coin in your collection, there are only three real reasons that should impact your decision. First: Was the coin acquired in a manner of importance to you or your family (passed down from your great-great–grandparents, for example, or obtained while serving in World War II)? Second: Is it a coin of importance to your collecting objective? This could be a coin that is part of an album you are trying to fill or a coin that contributes to a thematic objective such as Civil War memorabilia. Third: Is it a coin that you believe has a high probability of growing in value with time, and would like to keep for that reason?

If a coin passes none of those three tests, you should dispose of it. By answering all three of the above questions negatively, you have clearly categorized the coin as expendable. There is no point in keeping it; rather, it should be sold at fair value and the proceeds used for better purposes, whether related to your collecting pursuits or to meet some other need.

"Why consider method of sale now?" The purpose of this initial effort is to identify what items to keep and what items to dispose of. You may find later that there are parts of your collection that cannot be efficiently sold, due to the true cost of a transaction. This is a real issue that will not go away. If *you* do not resolve it, it will divert the efforts of your heirs and likely complicate the process for them. It is better to give coins away or turn them in at face value if there is no cost-effective sales approach that is worth your time. Once you know the full extent of the items to be sold, you will be in a better position to judge competing sales methodologies and select the best one for you.

"How can I identify investment potential?" Determining the investment potential of coins is a very difficult task. Depending on your level of interest and available time, you might wish to conduct some detailed research. Alternately, you could apply some broad guidelines to greatly reduce the amount of time you allocate to this task.

Historical-values charts are available for most U.S. coin types and may be used to determine past value changes as an estimate of future potential performance. For most coins, these tables show values that rise and fall over fairly long time periods. In some cases, a clear upward trend will be visible, but for many others that will not be the case. Coins that historically show consistent price appreciation, ignoring short- and medium-term fluctuations, may be identified as the best candidates for future growth. Depending on the series you collect, you may be able to view these historical value charts on the Internet or purchase historical values from pricing providers such as the *Coin Dealer Newsletter*. One option not requiring any expense is to assemble your own historical chart using annual value guides available over the time period of interest. You may have purchased such annually published guides as the Red Book, or you could browse such guides at a library.

You might not wish, however, to conduct a detailed historical analysis of value appreciation and instead apply some general guidelines. The following categories of coins are not likely to have significant potential for value appreciation:

- **Modern coins minted in large volumes.** Recent issues are typically minted in the millions with large quantities sold directly by the U.S. Mint to collectors. As a result many, many specimens remain in very high grades. Therefore it is very unlikely that many of these issues will appreciate in value. This includes all recent issues, including government sets (Proof sets, Uncirculated Mint sets) and commemorative coins. With a very few exceptions that were produced in abnormally low mintages, such as the 1995-W American Silver Eagle, most modern issues do not appreciate even to be worth the original issue price for very long periods of time.

- **Low-value coins such as poor-quality Indian Head cents and Buffalo nickels.** Even though these coins have some numismatic value, it is very difficult to sell them profitably due to the impact of transaction costs. If you choose to retain large quantities of such items, you should take care to understand their historical valuation.

While some Indian Head cents and Buffalo nickels can be quite valuable, typical dates in lower grades are not particularly collectible.

A Morgan dollar of a common date—such as this 1895—may hold numismatic value, but only rare-date coins in the series have a high likelihood of appreciating dramatically over time.

◆ ◆ ◆ ◆ ◆ ◆

- **Common-date collector coins (Morgan dollars, Mercury dimes, etc.).** Even though these coins have substantial numismatic value, their value growth may be quite limited. The base of active U.S. coin collectors has not grown in recent decades, and in fact the hobby population is demographically aging. As a result it is increasingly unlikely that the demand will increase relative to the supply.

- **Foreign coins.** Broadly speaking, collections of foreign coins can be divided into three categories: predominantly base-metal pocket-change coins accumulated as a result of travel or interaction with others; world bullion coins (gold, silver, platinum, and other precious metals); and specialized world-coin collections assembled by a knowledgeable collector focused in this area.

  If your foreign coins are essentially an accumulation of base-metal pocket change, you may find it difficult to obtain much value for them. The market for such coins is thinner than that for U.S. coins and price guides and other standard references might not exist. If your collection does contain pocket-change coins, you will want to check country-specific price guides if they are available.

  Foreign bullion coins such as Chinese Pandas, South African Krugerrands, Isle of Man Cats and Angels, Canadian Maple Leafs, British Britannias, Austrian Philharmonics, and Mexican Libertads have values that are tied to the spot prices of precious metals (the bullion value per ounce, of silver, gold, and platinum, as reported in the major markets). These coins are far easier to transact because they have standard weights (usually one ounce, or smaller fractions of an ounce) and standard fineness (for example, .999 fine silver). They are legal tender (though their denominations are far smaller than their precious-metal values) and their purity and weight is guaranteed by their issuing government, making them easily recognizable and confidently purchased and sold.

If you have specialized in a particular area of world-coin collecting (such as coins of Mexico, Canadian large cents, or crowns of the German States), it is very important that you pay special attention, as it is unlikely your heirs could properly dispose of or easily continue such a collection. You might choose to continue your focus on this area of collecting but should be sure to document the disposition or continuation of such a collection for your heirs.

Among foreign coins, those made of precious metal are the safest bet for holding actual value.

Among both U.S. and world issues, there are some easily identified coins with better potential for growth in value. Very simply stated, these are truly scarce coins that are always in short supply relative to demand. Typically they are coins that were minted in lower quantities than other date-and-mintmark varieties within their series. An example among modern issues is the 1995-W American Silver Eagle, which is worth thousands of dollars. It was produced only as a part of a special anniversary set consisting of four gold coins and the Silver Eagle. Its total mintage was 25,000, which is very small compared to the number of collectors who collect this series. Thus the U.S. Mint created an instant series key.

Unlike nearly every other American Silver Eagle, the 1995-W was produced only in the tens of thousands, making it the rarest in the series.

Older examples include such coins as the 1877 Indian Head cent, the 1942, 42 Over 41 Mercury dime overdate, and the 1895 Proof Morgan dollar. These were made or preserved in very small quantities compared to the collector bases of their series. It is such coins that have a long history of value growth.

Though past performance is not a guarantee of what is to come, you are far more likely to make good judgments if you are armed with historical performance data compiled over an extended time period. Some sources have suggested coins go up and down on periodic cycles. However, if you analyze coin prices over the last 50 years, such cycles are difficult to discern. There are temporary market bubbles that affect particular items. There are also unexpected impacts on supply and demand. One example is the discovery of a hoard of coins that significantly increases the available supply. Ultimately, the law of supply and demand does apply, and when the supply of a particular coin is significantly higher than the demand, its price it likely to fall.

	Mintage	F-12	VF-20	EF-40	MS-60	MS-63	MS-65	PF-65
1942, 42 Over 41 .... *		$625.00	$800.00	$1,000.00	$2,500	$4,500	$15,000	
1942.........(22,329)	205,410,000	2.25	3.10	3.25	6	12	30	$225
1942D, 42 Over 41 .... *		675.00	850.00	1,100.00	2,600	4,750	9,500	
1942D................	60,740,000	3.00	3.10	3.25	6	12	28	
1942S................	49,300,000	3.00	3.10	3.25	8	20	35	
1943................	191,710,000	3.00	3.10	3.25	6	12	27	
1943D................	71,949,000	3.00	3.10	3.25	6	15	30	
1943S................	60,400,000	3.00	3.10	3.25	7	16	30	
1944................	231,410,000	3.00	3.10	3.25	6	12	25	
1944D................	62,224,000	3.00	3.10	3.25	7	15	30	
1944S................	49,490,000	3.00	3.10	3.25	7	15	30	

Numismatic references such as the Red Book can help you determine what the "chase" coins in a series are; these are the most likely to appreciate in value over time.

✦ ✦ ✦ ✦ ✦

One other caution is that some guides suggest that rare coins will increase in value when other items such as stocks are going down. Such an analysis is greatly oversimplified. When stocks are falling rapidly, even affluent collectors may need cash and are sometimes forced to liquidate parts of their collections and/or reduce their buying activity. Forced liquidations and reduced spending simultaneously increase supply and reduce demand, likely resulting in a price drop.

FOCUSING ON THE FUTURE

Once you have decided on what coins you are going to keep and which ones you are going to liquidate, you are then in a position to focus your attention on two important matters.

You will want to allocate in an optimal manner those coins to be kept, with consideration of both your heirs and your desire for portions of the collection to be kept in the family. Later in this section you will receive detailed guidance on allocation.

Focus adequate attention on the sale of the items you have decided not to keep. Since these represent more value than those items liquidated in earlier bulk sales, it is likely that more of your time and effort is warranted in order to obtain an optimal result. Chapter 6 provides an overview of possible sales methodologies along with recommendations as to which work best for various parts of your collection.

*Align your collecting interests with your other goals,
both financial and personal.*

CHAPTER 4

Defining Your
Collection Objectives

Defining what objectives you seek to accomplish with your collection during retirement is critical to your continued enjoyment of the hobby. Your collecting focus should narrow greatly to specific collecting interests that are challenging and enjoyable. It is important that your collecting goals match realistically with your available time, money, and abilities.

You are the only person who can strike the optimal balance. This chapter is intended to provide you with an approach to defining these objectives.

The best place to start is to examine your current collection. Try to identify areas of the collection in which you have a high level of interest. There are several questions you may ask yourself to help focus your attention.

"Is there a portion of my collection that I consider incomplete and for which I also have a high level of interest?" Perhaps during your collecting years, you acquired a few California Gold Rush issues that have always piqued your interest. You might choose to define a specific collecting objective pertaining to California gold and use proceeds from the sale of the remainder of your collection to acquire the desired coins.

"Are there collecting objectives I have previously identified but been unable to pursue due to lack of time or funds?" Now in retirement you may be able to apply the needed time and also find the funds through consolidation of the remainder of your collection.

"Are there parts of my collection whose value could be dramatically improved by completing and/or upgrading portions?" Prior to sale by you or your heirs, it might be possible to enhance the value of a portion of your collection through a directed collecting effort.

Another avenue that may prove useful to defining your new collecting objectives is to consider your other interests and how they might intersect with coin collecting. Many other interests complement coin collecting.

HISTORICAL INTERESTS

You may be fascinated with the history of the world or specific periods or events. You might have interest in a particular wartime period such as the American Civil War, World War I, or World War II. Alternately you might focus on periods of great significance such as the Industrial Revolution, the California Gold Rush, Westward Expansion, or the American Revolution. If you have specialized historical interest, there are unlimited possibilities to combine coin collecting with the acquisition of other memorabilia while furthering your education.

The American Civil War. Interest in the American Civil War is very common. If you share such an interest, there are rich opportunities associated with this period. The Confederacy produced coins and paper currency. Civil War tokens, privately minted in bronze and the size of small cents, were produced commemorating various topics. A sample collecting objective might be to acquire one example of every U.S. coin issued from 1861 to 1865, from each mint. A less demanding objective would be to acquire one of each coin type. This could be combined with a collection of other Civil War artifacts such as military medals, arms, ammunition, and correspondence.

World War II. This war involved countries in all continents. Many coins were issued during wartime, often with special metallic content as a result of shortages produced by the war. You could collect all coins issued by direct participants in the war from 1939 or 1941 to 1945. You could identify a small set of the most significant coins and currency issued during this period.

A collection with a Civil War theme might include cent-sized tokens, coins struck by the Confederacy, or regular U.S. Mint issues from the time period (such as silver three-cent pieces like that pictured).

Alternately, you might establish a theme, collecting coins issued during 1941 to 1945 containing specific design elements such as eagles or military symbols. You might pursue a collection consisting of coins featuring the image of each major leader or military hero. Your coin-collecting activity could be coupled with collections of other items such as militaria, correspondence, or other items from a specific historical period.

A numismatic collection centered around World War II could include notes and coins of that time period from nations involved in that conflict.

California Gold Rush. If you have a historical interest in this period, you might define a collection spanning several issuers of California gold coinage, including a mixture of denominations and shapes. A collection might combine the coins of these mints along with other historical items associated with this period.

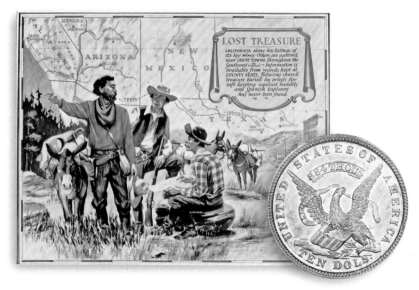

During the Gold Rush, both private minters and an official U.S. Assay Office minted gold coins of many different denominations.

• • • • •

American Revolution. This period enjoys substantial collector interest. Of course many of the coins issued during the Revolutionary era are relatively expensive, especially in high grades. You might define a type collection spanning the years leading up to the Revolutionary War as well as the first coins issued by the United States of America.

Collectors interested in the American Revolution might be attracted to any of a huge variety of coins, from Virginia halfpennies minted before the main armed conflict to Fugio coppers struck under the authority of the Continental Congress.

The Gilded Age. Many coin series with high collector interest were issued during the early 1900s. These include such types as Mercury dimes, Indian Head cents, Buffalo nickels, and Liberty Walking half dollars.

Coins like the Indian Head cent and Mercury dime are emblematic of the period Mark Twain dubbed the "Gilded Age."

✦ ✦ ✦ ✦ ✦

History of the United States Mints. If you have interest in the history of U.S. Mint facilities, you might seek to collect the first coin of each denomination issued by each mint. This could be extended to include the last coin of each denomination issued by mints that no longer exist.

Studying the history of the Mint and its facilities might spark a collector's imagination for a new collecting pursuit.

NUMISMATIC COLLECTIBLES OTHER THAN U.S. COINS

There are many numismatic collectibles other than coins minted by the United States government.

Tokens. Many organizations have minted tokens, typically made of base alloys and metals such as bronze or copper. Tokens were used in commerce for a variety of purposes. Transportation tokens, some still in use today, were made by many major systems such as the MBTA in Boston. These were purchased by travelers and used to pay for trains, subways, and buses. In the 1800s and 1900s many retail operations issued tokens good for purchases in their stores. Hard Times tokens were issued in the 1830s and 1840s when there were ongoing political and financial crises in the United States. These tokens are relatively inexpensive to collect and incorporate a variety of designs. Civil War tokens, mentioned previously, were issued depicting a variety of patriotic, military, and political topics. These are also very affordable to collect.

Transit tokens, Hard Times tokens, and Civil War tokens all have collector bases.

• • • • • ◆

Numismatic books. Over the years many hobby books have been published, some of which have become highly collectible. Early editions of the *Guide Book of United States Coins* (the annually issued "Red Book") and American Numismatic Association publications as well as some of the major works in the field are sought after by those interested in coin collecting.

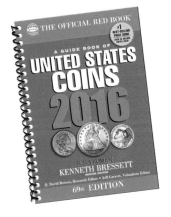

The chief numismatic reference book, the Red Book has itself become a collectible, with older editions having considerable value.

* * * * *

Colonial coins. Prior to the formation of the United States government, the British colonies and various private firms issued their own coins and tokens, mostly in copper, with some using precious metals. These coins dating from the early 1600s to the late 1700s span a major portion of the formative history of the United States. Many possible collecting themes can be identified based on geography, persons, colonial governments, and other parameters.

Many coins circulated in the British colonies, including Lord Baltimore six-pence such as this one.

* * * * *

FOREIGN COIN COLLECTIONS

Expanding coin collecting to include the entire world greatly increases the number of possibilities. There are almost an infinite number of potential collecting objectives.

Papal States. Coins associated with the Roman Catholic Church represent a wide swath of human history.

Princely States of India. India has a long history with significant representation in its numismatic items.

British Empire. For many decades Great Britain dominated world history with its influence reaching many areas of the globe. Many opportunities exist to define collecting objectives specific to the British Empire.

European Union. Since 1999, countries of the European Union have issued thousands of varieties of coins. You could define collecting objectives based on this period or alternately assemble a complete set of coins of each European Union member for the year immediately preceding their entry into the union.

Continent-specific collections. A collection can be formed consisting of all major coin types minted by countries of a specific continent such as South America or Africa.

A foreign coin collection could be focused on issues from anywhere in the world and from any time period in history.

* * * * *

THEMATIC COLLECTIONS

Another approach to your collecting would be to define a collection of coins whose art represents a specific theme.

Birds. Many coin issues depict birds such as eagles, hawks, and others. You could define a set of coins covering a set of countries and time periods that depict an eagle or other specific bird.

Animals. You might define a set of coins depicting certain animals such as dogs or horses.

People. A collection can be formed depicting heads of state or military leaders.

Maps. It is possible to collect coins that contain country, state, or city maps.

You might define a collection intended to help commemorate your career or travel history. You might collect a coin from each country visited with a date corresponding to the year of your visit.

Another thematic collection might be a set of coins intended to trace your family's ancestry as it moved around the globe.

The possibilities are only limited by your imagination. There is no end to the variety of possible thematic collecting objectives. Establishing a theme that is of high interest to you is the best way of setting meaningful collecting objectives that are likely to enhance your enjoyment.

GENERAL TIPS

It is important that your collecting pursuits be consistent with the funds that are likely to be available during your retirement. These funds might come from the sale of part of your collection or other assets. For example, the grades you seek for certain coins can dramatically affect their cost. Once you define your budget, you might seek to obtain a few key coins that are missing to complete some of your existing collections; or you might define an entirely new collecting goal requiring purchase of many coins, necessitating a more modest grade level.

Another important factor is availability of your time and the desired extent of your participation in the acquisition of new coins. If you are in good health and desiring more active participation, you can research an area of coin collecting very thoroughly, acquire a strong knowledge base, and use this to optimize your search. You might decide to travel to some major coin shows or auctions in order to play a direct role in locating coins of interest. If you don't want your participation to be that active, you might work with a local dealer to assist you in finding coins of interest. The more time available and the greater your participation, the greater your likely enjoyment.

Buying coins is very easy when you have adequate financial resources; however, selling your coins at fair value is much more challenging.

CHAPTER 5

For the Coin Collector: Selling Coins

You might, as is the case for most collectors, have relatively little experience selling coins. As a typical coin collector, you accumulated many coins over the years and never actually attempted to sell any of them. This lack of experience selling coins is unfortunate, as an understanding of the sales process makes you a better buyer of coins, often purchasing at much better prices. Many coin dealers have told me that they make most of their profit when they buy a coin, rather than when they sell it. The reason for this is that there are many dealers selling the same coins, so the prices that can be realized are set over a relatively small range. However, when you buy coins, there are many different situations that can result in great price differences.

For example, dealers often purchase raw coins (coins that are not certified by an independent third party) at grades that are conservative, as the dealer understandably does not want to take any grade risk when purchasing. (For example, a dealer might offer an MS-60 price for a raw Mint State coin that might grade MS-61 or MS-62 if later submitted for professional grading.) On average it is more likely that a raw coin will later be certified at a higher grade than the dealer estimated for offer purposes, rather than at a lower grade. A single grade-step increase can substantially affect the value of a coin, sometimes increasing its value by more than 100%.

It is never too late to learn. An understanding of the sales process will make you better prepared to estimate the realizable value of portions of your collection as well as the extent of the task to be faced by your family as they attempt to dispose of your coins. Your knowledge of coin collecting leaves you much better prepared, and as you learn how selling coins works, it will likely affect your decisions as to what to keep. If you continue to acquire coins, you will do so in a more cost-effective manner.

Sale of those items you have identified will benefit you and your heirs in several ways:

- You will reduce the number of items that they have to store and sell, enabling them to focus on obtaining maximum value from a smaller number of items.
- You will avoid potential conflicts due to inequitable distribution of items whose true value is not well understood.
- The proceeds of your estate will not be delayed pending sales of coins.
- Your continued enjoyment of your collection will be enhanced as you focus on portions that are of greater interest, with additional resources freed up by disposition of less important items.

You should approach the task of selling coins with the same enthusiasm as collecting the coins in the first place. View this as a learning exercise that will make you a better collector. It is an opportunity for you to explore and participate in new aspects of coin collecting. You will have the opportunity to meet and interact with new collectors and dealers in a variety of settings.

Properly researching your potential sales methods and maximizing your profits will make matters easier for your heirs, provide you with peace of mind, and allow you to appreciate a different aspect of coin collecting.

CASE STUDY:
JIM LEARNS ABOUT SELLING COINS

Like many collectors, Jim had been collecting coins for many years but had never attempted to sell any of them. He had maintained an inventory of his collection and had listed the market values obtained from various price guides, but always wondered what he would be able to obtain in an actual sale.

After retiring, Jim realized that he needed to understand the possible approaches to selling coins and the real values he might obtain. He started by reading online articles and speaking to other collectors about transacting coins. This initial research opened Jim's eyes to the complexity of selling coins as well as the variety of approaches.

He decided to conduct a more detailed bit of research to gain a more precise understanding of the value of his collection using different sales methods. Jim started with some online research regarding coin auctions. He assembled a few coins from his collection representing a cross section and began searching auction records to locate recent sales. He searched eBay sales and also professional coin auctions.

As a result of this initial research, he was able to compare real auction results with the market values published in price guides. Being thorough, Jim also accounted for the transaction costs such as auction fees, certification fees, and shipping charges.

Jim also purchased current issues of weekly numismatic publications and scoured them for buy ads from a variety of coin dealers. He compared the buy prices with those listed in the value guides and also his analysis of auction results.

After reviewing what he had already learned, Jim was able to divide his collection into various portions based on the best liquidation method. He also separated some items of higher value for which he had not yet identified an acceptable sales approach.

For those items of higher value, Jim decided to approach a local coin dealer about a consignment sale. The dealer would sell the coins for Jim with an agreed-upon minimum price and profit participation. Jim decided to provide a profit with a built-in incentive for a higher price. He also consigned a few of his more expensive coins to a major auction house.

After having sold coins through a variety of approaches, Jim not only learned how to obtain the best values for his coins, but also acquired the knowledge of how to acquire coins more cost-effectively. This would be of great value as he pursued his new collecting objectives.

MAKE THE METHOD RIGHT FOR YOU

Selling coins is complicated by the variety of approaches that produce widely varying results. One particular approach might not work well for an entire typical collection. Your collection should be sold in sections using the optimal method for each. The remainder of this chapter provides some insight into the challenges of selling certain types of coins. It is not intended to be a comprehensive analysis of all possible sales methodologies. Rather it is intended to provide you with some basic understanding of the parameters involved and assist in starting the thought process.

Before you begin, it is important to reflect on your likely interest and enjoyment of the sales process. You also have to decide what value, if any, you will place on your time. For some collectors (for example, who are not engaged in income-generating activities and who enjoy coin collecting as a hobby), the decision will be to place no value on their time. Others might have the opportunity to spend their time on activities that are more profitable or enjoyable and will therefore want to assign a cost to time spent selling coins.

The remainder of this chapter will treat the following categories of coins separately:

- Truly rare/scarce coins of higher value
- Mid-range-value common collector coins
- Low-value collector coins
- Complete sets
- U.S. government sets
- Coins worth bullion value
- Foreign coins

Disclaimer: *The discussion of sales methods throughout the remainder of this section is intended to make you aware of the possibilities rather than instruct you how to sell each type of coin. The best approach and available venues may change with time and you need to select approaches consistent with your skills. When you actu-*

ally go to sell some coins, you should explore all possible alternative sales tech-niques, consistent with the amount of time you are willing to devote, and first conduct a few smaller transactions to gain experience with selling effectively.

TRULY RARE/SCARCE COINS OF HIGHER VALUE ($1,000+)

If you are fortunate to have coins worth $1,000 or more apiece, they likely represent a major portion of the realizable value from your collection. Additionally, they have the best potential for value growth. Since these items are of higher value, your attention should be focused on them first.

Items in this category must be certified so that the basis of the valuation (the grade of the coin) does not introduce uncertainty into the value. It is recommended that such coins be certified by ANACS, NGC, or PCGS, the three largest third-party professional grading companies, which are well known and respected by most coin dealers. Once you know the grade of the coin, you will understand the retail and wholesale valuations and be prepared to negotiate the terms of a fair transaction.

Prior to selling high-value coins, you should be aware of both retail and wholesale pricing. *Coin World Values,* published in the monthly magazine installment of *Coin World,* presents a good estimate of retail pricing simi-lar to the Red Book but more frequently updated. The *Coin Dealer News-letter* ("Greysheet") is an excellent reference for wholesale pricing. There often is a large spread between these wholesale-retail values, which nar-rows considerably for truly scarce items in great demand. If a coin dealer-ship has a customer waiting for a hard-to-find coin and is presented with an opportunity to purchase it, they will likely be willing to buy very close to retail as their money will not be tied up in inventory and they are not taking risk holding onto the coin.

One approach to selling high-value rare coins is to involve a significant auction house which will market them. This is most attractive when you have sufficient such items to gain adequate attention from a major auc-tion house. Typically, this route would be appropriate for a collection worth $25,000 or more, concentrated on a small number of high-value coins. Auctions are also appropriate for high-value single coins that are in demand (typically an individual coin worth $10,000 or more).

A second approach, one that works very well when the number of items is not quite sufficient for an auction house, is a consignment sale. This involves selecting a coin dealer who will market your coins for an agreed-upon fee on a consignment basis. In this method, the dealer does not take on inventory risk and only receives compensation when the item is

A Flowing Hair dollar from 1795, a high-value coin appropriate for a consignment sale or auction.

• • • • • •

sold. If realistic terms are agreed upon, the dealer has incentive to sell the coin as quickly as possible at the highest price possible.

A recommended approach is to discuss and reach agreement on a realistic price objective and then provide the dealer with a strong incentive if a higher price is realized. For example, if a dealer believes he can quickly sell a coin at $8,000, you might agree on a 10% commission on sale at $8,000, with the dealer receiving 25 to 33% of any amount over $8,000. If the coin were sold for $10,000 the dealer would receive $800 (10%) + $500 (25% of excess over $8,000).

Arranging a consignment sale with a dealer you trust can lead to excellent returns.

Using such an approach, the dealer is assured that his time will not be wasted since he can sell it at a marketable price, but he is also incented to place some effort into selling at a premium price.

Consignment sales will often produce the best return; however, they often result in delayed payment. For example, if the dealer holds the coin for 30 to 60 days while it is being sold, you will not be paid until the dealer has received payment and also any return period has expired. This means that a 60- to 90-day period is likely to occur between the coin being consigned and your receiving payment.

One caution with respect to consignment sales is to make sure that your coin is protected from loss if anything happens affecting the dealer or their business. Some coin dealers are one-person businesses that might collapse if the dealer becomes ill or passes away. Others are operating on tight cash flows and in the event of a downturn could go bankrupt. You want to be sure that you have no exposure to loss during the period in which the dealer has possession of the coin and you are paid for it.

The best approach is to select a dealer with a long, successful history in the coin market, through good and bad cycles. You should also discuss this issue during your consignment negotiations so that ownership of the coin clearly remains with you until you are paid.

A third approach for these items is outright sale to a dealer. In this instance, the dealer is taking on inventory risk. His funds are tied up for the length of time that passes between the acquisition and subsequent sale of the coin. Also, if the market prices should drop during this interval, there is a risk of loss. As a result of taking on these risks, it is likely that the dealer will require a higher percentage.

The primary advantage of this approach is certainty and quick payment. Usually you receive a check from the dealer on the day you deliver the coin, and thus you don't need to wait for payment and/or take on any risk of loss during a consignment period. Generally speaking, this approach is best for coins the dealer is confident he can sell quickly, as he minimizes his inventory risk in that case. A best-case would be when a dealer has a specific customer who has asked him to locate the coin you are selling so that he can sell it immediately.

If you are going to take this approach, you should make sure that any individual coins worth more than $100 are certified so that grade risk is not a part of the equation. No sensible dealer would assume any grade risk, thus their only sensible course is to acquire the coin at a grade that they are confident it will meet. This means that if the coins are not certified, you could potentially be selling some coins below their real grades.

Mid-Range Value
Common Collector Coins

Your collection may contain many individual coins worth $50 to $500 apiece that are commonly available. For example, you might have a collection of common-date Morgan dollars in various grades.

Two coins that fall into the "mid-range value" category: an 1832 half dollar in AU-58 and an 1893 Isabella commemorative quarter in MS-61.

. . . . . .

Your coins in this category may have a considerable aggregate value. For example, if you have 200 coins with an average retail value of $300 each, the retail aggregate would be $60,000. The problem is that such coins are readily available and often already held in the inventories of dealers with whom you might do business. If, for example, you have a common-date Morgan dollar graded MS-65 that is worth $250, but the dealers you survey already have that coin in inventory, they are going to want to purchase substantially below retail (perhaps 30 to 40%) since they will likely hold the coin for a while and have to discount the sales price. Thus, your return on these items is likely to be significantly lower than retail, perhaps 60 to 75% of retail as typical.

There are a couple of relatively easy approaches to selling these coins. One is outright sale to a dealer. If you are satisfied with the proceeds of an offer, this results in the quickest payment. This is also easiest, but it probably produces the poorest return. If you do take this approach, you should obtain a current copy of the *Coin Dealer Newsletter* ("Greysheet").

The offer from the dealer should be around the Greysheet's "bid" price, which is typically 25 to 35% below retail pricing. If you receive an offer at Greysheet bid price and wish to complete a quick and easy cash transaction, such an approach is a good option. If you are receiving an offer below Greysheet bid value, it would be advisable to offer these coins to other dealers.

What about eBay, you ask? eBay serves as the venue for a very high volume of online coin-related transactions. If you are considering selling some of your coins on eBay, you will want to do some research, so that you understand what works, eBay's rules for selling coins in its auctions, and also what coins are likely to be sold at a good return. There is a separate chapter in section III of this book which addresses this topic in more detail.

eBay is a popular sales venue for coins, but conducting business via this outlet can be complicated.

• • • • •

An alternative approach is a professional online coin auction. There are a number of houses that offer such auctions, such as Stacks Bowers Galleries (stacksbowers.com) and Heritage Auctions (ha.com), and they can garner widespread participation. Most such services allow you to view the history of earlier auctions. By searching these archives, you can likely find coins of the same type, date, and grade that sold recently so you can come up with a good estimate of your potential net proceeds. Also, if you have coins which are not yet certified, some auction houses include certification in the sales process. Since they certify thousands of coins, they can offer this service at a lower rate than other companies and thus provide for collectors a more cost-effective approach than submitting coins to a third-party certification service before consigning them to auction.

A third possibility is to combine these approaches: analyze recent online auctions to determine the probable net proceeds you would receive and then use that information to negotiate a direct sale with a dealer. You should take this approach with an understanding that you will likely receive smaller proceeds in return for quicker, certain payment.

Finally, a few straightforward recommendations before moving on from the mid-range–value category. For higher-value coins within this segment, work with auction houses and coin-dealer firms populated by professional numismatists who engage in transactions with serious coin collectors. This is likely to yield the best results in most circumstances. eBay is the "Wild West" of coin auctions, with participants including buyers and sellers who don't know much about coin collecting or what they are doing. There are also a small percentage of sellers who misrepresent the items they are offering.

For many pre-1964 collector coins, eBay auctions do not typically generate returns higher than Greysheet bid prices after consideration of the auction fees, and therefore such higher-value items are usually better disposed of by outright sale to a dealer at Greysheet bid price or consignment sale. One exception to this tip relates to modern coins. Many modern coins are sold on eBay at higher prices than would be expected—perhaps there are many bidders who are not serious numismatists and are unaware of coin valuations. If you do decide to sell on eBay, read and thoroughly understand chapter 17, "Selling on eBay for Enjoyment or Profit."

To summarize, selling via online auction is likely to produce higher proceeds with a slightly larger effort and delayed payment, whereas a dealer transaction will result in a lower immediate payment with minimal effort. If your coins are not certified, auction houses that include certification with their services may provide a strong benefit, as you will otherwise have to bear certification costs at retail rates or accept a dealer's offer at the value of the coin's "lowest possible" grade.

SPECIAL SECTION: PRICING GUIDES

There are many price guides available in print form or accessible on the Internet. It is important to have a basic understanding of what guides are most commonly used.

A Guide Book of United States Coins (the "Red Book"), *Coin World Values,* and others. These are retail price guides intended to provide prices that collectors can expect to pay for coins. Such prices, however, are only a guide. The actual price a collector pays will vary based on where he buys the coin and how scarce it really is.

Coin Dealer Newsletter's "Greysheet." This guide provides the prices at which coin dealers are buying and selling coins. If you are buying expensive coins, you should be aware of these values and how they compare to those presented in retail guides. Typically, Greysheet prices, both for buying and for selling (called "bid" and "ask"), are significantly below retail values. This gap should narrow for coins that are more expensive and/or scarce. If you are buying a $100 coin, the transaction costs will require a significant difference between the bid and ask pricing of the dealer. However, for more expensive items, a fair profit on the transaction can occur with a smaller difference. Whenever you buy a coin at higher than the Greysheet's asked price, you should have a clear reason for doing so.

A Handbook of United States Coins (the "Blue Book"). This guide is similar to the Red Book, but instead of providing prices collectors can expect to pay, it contains wholesale or buy pricing.

Online guides. There are a variety of online price guides for United States coins and world coins. Coin World's Web site (coinworld.com) is one of the more prominent resources which is considered independent. Note that some online price guides are authored by organizations with some interest in the coins that are valued.

LOW-VALUE COLLECTOR COINS

Quite often collectors have boxes or other containers filled with low-grade, low-value coins. Typically found are Lincoln Wheat cents, Indian Head cents, Buffalo nickels, Eisenhower dollars, etc. This portion of a collection often takes up a lot of space, yet it makes up a small portion of a collection's overall value. Excluded from this category are coins with silver and gold content or key dates which should be separated out.

The estimates provided by value guides for low-value, low-grade coins do not reflect their real value if sold or their replacement value for insurance purposes. For example, you might have 200 miscellaneous well-worn, common-date Indian Head cents, on which a guide might place an average value of $1. That might lead you to believe the value of these pieces totals $200. The problem is that these items are commonly available, and the cost of a transaction is a significant portion of the value. A coin dealer cannot afford to spend an hour of time selling 200 Indian Head cents, nor 30 minutes meeting with you to discuss sales approaches.

Even if you place no value on your time, you might incur shipping or other expenses related to your efforts to sell such items. The bottom line here is that these items typically represent a small portion of your collection's value, and thus you won't want to spend a lot of time on them.

Factor in transaction costs when evaluating collections of low-value, low-grade coins like these Indian Head cents.

Probably the best option for sale of these items it to look in the back of an issue of *Coin World, Numismatic News,* or a similar publication. There you will find dealer's buy prices for bulk shipments of such items. While these prices are typically in the vicinity of 50% of retail pricing, all that is required of you is to place your low-value coins in a box, take it to the post office, and pay modest postage and insurance charges. A week or so later, you will receive a check in the mail.

Alternately, the total value might be small enough that you feel comfortable gifting these coins to a budding collector as your contribution to the growth of coin collecting.

COMPLETE SETS

One special case involving low-value coins is if you have accumulated a complete set (or nearly complete) set. For example, you might have an Indian Head cent album filled with low-grade specimens of all dates (or all except one). Such items are a bit easier to sell and less commonly held in inventory, and therefore direct sale to a dealer—or perhaps an eBay auction—might be a viable approach.

If, however, you have a complete collection of high-value, well-matched coins in higher grades, approaches similar to selling high-value individual coins would be more appropriate.

Complete sets of low-value coins such as State quarters can be easier to sell than the individual coins.

GOVERNMENT-ISSUED SETS

Like many collectors, you may have purchased annual coin sets (Proof sets, Mint sets, or commemorative sets) regularly from the United States Mint. Though these items are attractively packaged and often relatively inexpensive to purchase, most are valued below their original cost for a very long period of time. Such items are made in large quantities (millions), kept intact by collectors for many years, and never become scarce. The supply is always adequate to meet the demand, resulting in low market pricing.

You may overestimate the value of such items and be greatly disappointed by sales proceeds. Realistically, such items are low-value commodities and might be best sold using the same approach as low-value coins. Typically, you'll want to view the "wanted" section of a weekly numismatic publication and mail them to the buyer with the highest buy prices.

There have been a few exceptions, though, in the cases of these sets containing coins with very low mintages relative to the collector base. Notable among these is the 1995-W American Silver Eagle; only 25,000 were minted, as it was only available as a part of a five-coin set that

A Proof set from 1990 with a "No S" Lincoln cent would be among the rare government-issued sets that are valued far above their original issue price.

included four gold American Eagle coins (1/10-oz., 1/4-oz., 1/2-oz., and 1-oz.). The sets were offered to collectors for about $1,000, whereas the individual Silver Eagles were usually purchased for about $20. Between the limited supply, prohibitively high price point, and large population of Silver Eagle collectors, there was nowhere for the price to go but up. Recently, examples of this coin graded from PF-65 to PF-69 have realized values between $3,000 and $6,000. PF-70 specimens have sold for $20,000.

Other special issues, such as the Reverse Proof Silver Eagles of 2011, have appreciated to a value of a few hundred dollars in a short period of time. Another recent example of rapid growth in value is the 25th anniversary Silver Eagle set, which contained five coins including a Reverse Proof and an S-mintmark Eagle. This set, offered by the Mint at $250, sold out and immediately rose to a value of more than $600.

Reverse Proof American Silver Eagles, such as the one released in 2011, have appreciated quickly.

✦ ✦ ✦ ✦ ✦

Another category of recent issues that appreciated substantially is coins with minting errors. For example, the Presidential dollar series had a number of issues with no edge lettering. These coins command prices many times those of the normal coins. The State quarter issues also included a number of error coins, some of which resulted in extra features in the design. At least some of these error coins also command hundreds of dollars, as there are many State quarter collectors who wish to assemble a complete set including errors.

COINS WORTH BULLION VALUE

Coins with substantial gold and/or silver content and no significant numismatic premium are very easy to value and sell. Standard tables exist which provide the fineness and weight of metal content of most coins, so the precious metal value can be precisely calculated based on current spot prices.

Of course, when you go to sell, there will be some transaction costs, thus preventing you from receiving 100% of the precious-metal value. Generally, the higher quantity of pieces you have for sale and the closer you are to the metal refiner, the closer you can get to full value. Conversely, the more middlemen involved in the transaction, the lower your proceeds.

Selling gold and silver to mall jewelry stores usually results in the poorest returns, often 50% or less. If you go into such a transaction without an understanding of what value would constitute a 100% return, you are relying on the store to accurately estimate the precious-metal content. Also, a store operator must cover the overhead of having a storefront and thus must be able to make a certain amount of profit off the transaction.

Selling your coins that have precious-metal content to a jewelry or pawn shop typically results in poor returns.

❖ ❖ ❖ ❖ ❖

The bottom line is that if you have coins worth bullion value, you should know their exact bullion content. You should also be aware of the current spot price on the day you are going to sell. With this information, you are armed with the knowledge to get the best price. Smaller quantities might be sold at a 5 to 15% discount on the spot price, whereas larger quantities might be transacted at a discount of 1 to 5% of spot price. The profit for the refiner/dealer must be sufficient to justify the transaction as well as handling/processing of the item. Larger quantities enable the dealer to realize their profit objectives with a smaller overhead cost.

When estimating the value of your bullion coins, special attention needs to be given to older, worn, low-value silver coins. For example, if you have highly worn older dimes, quarters, and half dollars of poor quality, significant parts of the metal weight may be gone. This physical loss of mass can be seen with the naked eye: if you stack 50 old dimes next to 50 modern dimes, you will often notice the stack of older dimes is substantially shorter as a result of the material lost to wear.

Thus, you will want to weigh a group of such coins and compare your weight to that of the original coins in order to estimate the value of such items. You should then reduce the bullion estimate by this percentage. For example, if you have 100 silver dimes which the catalog indicates should weigh 2.5 grams each, you can calculate that the total weight of unworn, full-weight coins would be 250 grams. If you weigh your coins as a group and the scale reads 225 grams, then the bullion content of your coins should be multiplied by .90 to account for the metal lost due to wear.

If you have a substantial quantity of precious metal and a local dealer who handles a large volume of bullion coins, you should be able to negotiate a price discounted from the spot price by a very low percentage that still provides adequate compensation for time spent by the dealer in handling the transaction. It is best to work with dealers with a close relationship to a refiner, such that they can immediately turn around the coins and thereby incur no inventory risk and not tie up cash. Keep in mind the coin dealer will also bundle bullion purchases from several customers into a larger transaction with the refiner, enabling him to receive a higher value than the collector. In this way, everyone wins, as the collector is able to receive proceeds similar to that realizable in a direct transaction with a refiner while the dealer receives a small profit based on his ability to combine several small bullion purchases into one larger transaction with the refiner.

For smaller quantities, the best result is probably obtained by directly mailing your items to a refiner. You might also be able to mail them to a dealer who advertises competitive prices for bullion purchases (he is likely able to offer these prices because he is effectively bundling transactions for sale to a refiner).

If you have items manufactured by private mints which are made of solid silver, gold, or another precious metal, these are usually valued at bullion value and best sold in a manner similar to U.S. coins valued based on bullion prices. Be aware that *plated* coins usually contain very little precious metal and are usually worthless. A gold-plated one-ounce coin, for example, might contain pennies worth of gold—even when the spot price of gold is $1,000 or even $2,000 per ounce. Gold- or silver-plated items made by private mints should be perceived as having no market value and only collected to satisfy personal collecting interests.

Gold-plated medals like this "slug" made to commemorate the discovery of gold in California in 1848 often do not have significant precious-metal content.

* * * * *

FOREIGN COINS

Valuing and selling foreign coins can be more difficult than doing the same with U.S. coins (with the exception of coins worth bullion value, which should be approached in the same as U.S. bullion coins). Common foreign bullion coins include South African Krugerrands, Canadian Maple Leafs, Chinese Pandas, Isle of Man Cats and Angels, Mexican Libertads, Austrian Philharmonics, Australian Lunars, British Britannias, and Russian Chervonetz. The fineness (percentage of precious metal) of these issues varies, and when valuing them you must take into account this ratio in order to calculate the fair market value.

If you have specialized in an area of foreign-coin collecting, you will want to be sure to thoroughly research their value. A starting point is to determine if there is a country-specific price guide for the coins you collect. A second step is to find coin dealers who specialize in buying and selling such coins.

With respect to foreign coins which do not contain precious metal or for which there is numismatic value above the bullion value, determining fair value is similar to valuing U.S. coins. Some value guides covering multiple countries greatly overstate foreign coin valuations. As a result, you are likely to face disappointment if you attempt to sell coins based on these values. Most base-metal issues (those of copper, nickel, steel, and alloys) from around the world are worth very little and cannot be sold for a profit. It is usually best to gift these to an interested young collector. The best estimates of numismatic value for foreign coins are obtained from country-specific guides, if available. But even with these guides, collector markets are generally smaller, and professional help from a qualified dealer will make it easier to sell to these markets.

If you have a collection of low-value base-metal (copper, nickel, bronze, etc.) foreign coins, your best approach for dispersal of these pieces is probably to give them to a budding collector. Young collectors enjoy seeing and studying the variety of coin designs used throughout the world.

If you have a collection of high-value items, it might be best to work directly with a dealer specializing in coins of the countries you collect.

Base-metal foreign coins make for a great gift to a young collector.

TO SUMMARIZE

Selling a coin collection can be hard. It is not like selling stocks and bonds, which can be transacted in a few seconds with low transaction costs and at a more or less universal price. When it comes to selling coins, the more knowledge you apply, the better your outcome will be. Depending on your enjoyment of the sales process and willingness to spend your time pursuing it, there may be portions from which no real value can be realized, and these might be best given away. How much time you spend is up to you, and you should base your decision on your enjoyment as well as the opportunity cost associated with your allocation of time.

Whatever amount of time you decide to spend, it is best to start where the value is concentrated and work your way down. In this way, you will realize the best overall return, and if you get tired along the way and decide to abandon the remainder of the process, what remains will be the lower-value portions of your collection. As a result, you will probably have achieved the highest possible return based on the amount of time you were willing to expend.

SPECIAL SECTION: WHAT COINS SHOULD BE CERTIFIED

Several decades ago, a number of companies began offering certification services for coins. These companies professionally authenticate a coin, grade its condition and place it in a sealed container, or "slab"—basically, a plastic holder with a label identifying the coin and its grade. More recently, embedded security features have been implemented in the slabs' designs in order to prevent forged copies of the slabs themselves. Certified coins from reputable companies eliminate most of the issue of determining the condition of a coin and also validate its authenticity. A certified coin is more marketable, and the owner is more capable of estimating a fair value in the event of a sale.

It is important, however, that the certification service used is considered reputable, as coins certified by certain other companies are no easier to deal with than raw coins. Also note that owners assigning grades to their own coins and placing them in plastic holders is sometimes useful to buyers as a starting point, but a knowledgeable collector knows that such coins are effectively raw coins as far as the marketplace is concerned.

When preparing a collection for sale, most collectors will encounter hundreds of coins which are not certified by a third party. The grade for these coins may not be known or may have been assigned by either the dealer from whom they were purchased or the collector him or herself. Regardless of how this unofficial grade was determined, such items will not necessarily be assumed to be the grade they are marked by the purchasing dealer, as it would be unwise for them to take on grade risk.

Certification is not inexpensive and is not worth doing for every coin. For example, if you have a coin worth $25 in Very Good condition and $40 in Fine, and the dealer offers you $20 for it (80% of the Very Good price), it would not be worth it to certify the coin at Fine at a cost of $15 and then receive $32 from the dealer. That would yield a profit of just $17, whereas taking the dealer's initial offer and selling it uncertified yields $20. In addition, payment would be delayed by several weeks by the certification process.

You must decide what coins are worth certification. A recommended strategy is to look at the value guides, specifically the differences in prices at various grades. Examine the value one grade lower and one grade higher than that currently assigned to the coin. If the value differences are similar in magnitude to the cost of certification, it is not worthwhile to pay the costs associated with certification. If, on the other hand, the value differences are several multiples of the certification cost, certification may be worthwhile.

For coins that have not yet been certified, estimate a grade range and check the price points along that range. Sometimes, the increase in value for being graded higher may not be enough to make up for the cost of certification; for example, an 1855 Liberty Seated quarter in VF-20 is only valued $10 higher than one in F-12 (per Red Book 2017 prices).

The recommended approach follows several steps. First take a representative small sample of coins (perhaps 10 to 15 coins), and make up a spreadsheet including the values at the assigned grade, one grade higher, and one grade lower. Then send these coins for certification. This will probably cost around $200. Next compare the expected values of the uncertified coins versus those of the certified ones. For coins worth less than $200 each, an approximate expected value prior to certification might be 75 to 80% of the average of the assigned grade's value and that of the grade below. Meanwhile, the value of the certified coins might be 75 to 80% of the retail value of the assigned grade. If the value of the certified coins exceeds the value of the raw coins by an amount greater than the certification cost, then the certification was justified and you can send in the next batch.

An example to further illustrate this process and its potential benefits: Suppose you sent in 10 coins estimated at MS-63, and each had a market value at that grade of about $160, for a total value of $1,600. You received back from the certification service one coin graded MS-62, seven graded MS-63, and two graded MS-64. The one graded MS-62 lost $50 in expected value due to being graded lower than expected, but the two graded MS-64 rose by $250 in expected value each, resulting in a gain of $450. The certification cost was about $150, so by certifying these coins you increased the estimated market value net of certification cost by about $300. You also confirmed the seven MS-63 assignments, eliminating the grade risk if you decide to sell.

Depending on how many coins in total you are dealing with, you might send coins off for certification in larger batches. Basically, you would continue until all coins are sold and/or the effort is not producing desirable results. A benefit of this approach is that you can be selling coins all along the way and using part of the proceeds to pay for the certification cost of the next batch.

If you do decide to have your coins certified, it is important to make sure you are using companies whose certifications are generally accepted by the market as being fair, consistent, and accurate. Currently PCGS (Professional Coin Grading Service) and NGC (Numismatic Guaranty Corporation of America) are widely accepted by most dealers and collectors. ANACS (formerly the

NGC, PCGS, ICG, and ANACS are the most respected third-party certification companies.

✦ ✦ ✦ ✦ ✦

official certification service of the American Numismatic Association) and ICG (Independent Coin Graders) are also widely accepted by many dealers and collectors. ANACS is widely respected for circulated coinage and ICG for modern coins. When you choose your certification company be very careful as many of the competitors that are not well accepted have names very similar to those above.

If you have coins that were certified by a company other than NGC, PCGS, ANACS, or ICG, it is very possible that the assigned grade will not be accepted by the market and you may need to have the coin recertified in order to maximize your return. One strategy is to take the coin to a local dealer and ask if they would purchase it at the grade represented and, if they would not, what they believe the grade of the coin to actually be. If you do this with a few dealers (or one dealer with whom you have an established relationship), you should be able to get sufficient guidance to determine which coins need to be graded again. It is very possible that the actual grades will be many steps less than that assigned grade, resulting in a value which is a fraction of the value at the originally assigned grade.

Finally, if you have access to a trusted dealer, you might "prescreen" your coins—that is, seek their guidance as to what coins should be considered for certification. A knowledgeable dealer should be able to grade sufficiently close to know if the likely grade warrants the cost of certification.

CASE STUDY: CERTIFYING A COIN PRIOR TO A TRANSACTION

Ralph had been collecting coins for many years. His collection contained two key coins that were the most valuable, an 1852 Liberty Head double eagle and a 1909 Saint-Gaudens double eagle. Both coins had been gifts from his father. The coins were not professionally graded, but Ralph thought them both to be Mint State (Uncirculated). Ralph looked up their values in a current price guide and noted that the market value of the 1852 coin ranged from $6,500 in MS-60 to $42,500 in MS-64. Meanwhile the 1909 coin had a value ranging from $1,650 in MS-60 to $8,500 in MS-64.

Ralph took these coins to a local dealer with whom he had conducted many coin transactions. The dealer indicated a willingness to purchase the coins at a price about twice the MS-60 value. He also indicated to Ralph that these coins could grade higher but that he could not take the risk of assuming a higher grade. The dealer advised Ralph that if he were willing to pay the certi-

Ralph's careful, logical approach to having his
coins graded paid off.

✦ ✦ ✦ ✦ ✦

fication fee (several hundred dollars), sending the coin to NGC
or PCGS would allow Ralph to have confidence that he was
receiving a fair price for the coin. Ralph agreed and authorized
the dealer to have the two coins certified.

After waiting several weeks, the certified coins were returned
to Ralph's dealer. The 1909 coin was assigned a grade of MS-64,
which the retail guides valued at $8,500. The 1852 was assigned
MS-62, which the guides valued at $16,500. Based on these
grades, the dealer offered to purchase the coins at prices substantially higher than those originally offered and closer to the
coins' true market value. Ralph's investment in certification and
willingness to wait a few weeks for the results proved to be very
worthwhile, as the price he could obtain for these coins had
more than doubled. His willingness to bear the cost of certification and eliminate the grade risk prior to a transaction enabled
him to make a much larger profit than if he had sold the coins
uncertified.

SPECIAL SECTION:
WORKING WITH A COIN DEALER
TO SELL YOUR COLLECTION

A coin dealer can provide significant guidance to facilitate your coin sales and also participate in the transactions. Of course, capitalizing on this expertise requires that you establish a working relationship and mutual trust with a dealer. Establishing such a relationship takes time and is accomplished through a sequence of steps which builds sufficient trust so that you can rely on the dealer's guidance.

One critical component of such a relationship is that you acquire sufficient knowledge of what you are doing; that way, you can effectively evaluate what you are told by the dealer, ask intelligent questions, pose sensible alternatives, and earn the respect of the dealer. In turn, the dealer must earn your trust and respect by demonstrating that he will properly honor your interests in any transactions.

If you can establish an effective working relationship, the time required to complete your sales should be greatly diminished. Some items may be sold directly to the dealer. Conversely, the dealer may identify some items which are better sold through a different approach, and he should be able to provide some guidance in choosing which method of sale is best. As mentioned earlier, a dealer should also be able to provide guidance as to what coins warrant certification.

Another area in which a dealer can provide assistance is in the valuation of the coins in an estate. It is often necessary to establish the value as of the date of the collectors' death. A knowledgeable coin dealer can assist with such a valuation.

It takes time to build confidence in such a relationship, and this is best accomplished through a sequence of transactions which start small and increase in value as confidence and trust grows. The early transactions should be conducted with an objective of building confidence. This is where acquisition of knowledge on your part is essential. Below are a few sample confidence-building transactions.

Sample confidence-building transaction 1. You might select 10 coins from your collection which you believe to be worth $200 to $500 based on the grades you have assigned. You might then take these to a dealer and offer them for sale. Ask for both the dealer's buy price for each coin and his grade assumptions. Then submit the coins for certification by NGC or PCGS and compare the assigned grades with those assumed by the dealer as well as the prices he is willing to pay with Greysheet bid prices.

Sample confidence-building transaction 2. Select a group of low-grade coins worth bullion value. Look in the back of an issue of *Coin World* for the best buy prices for silver and assemble a group of silver coins which you could sell for $500 to $1,000. Take these to the dealer and see what offer you are made. Compare it against selling to the mail-order dealer with appropriate consideration of the fact that you save mailing expense and receive an immediate check from your local dealer should you take his offer.

Sample confidence-building transaction 3. Take a few lower-value items and ask for an offer from the dealer. Then take those items and sell them via auction on eBay.

View favorably any efforts made by the dealer to educate you on the way in which to obtain the best price for your coins. View with caution any pressure to sell the coins quickly, as no one knows what fluctuations will occur in the market, and they usually occur slowly.

One other consideration with respect to selection of a coin dealer is their membership in the Professional Numismatists Guild (PNG). Dealers that are members have agreed to adhere to ethical standards and are more likely to have established businesses that will remain in existence. This is not, however, a guarantee that you will receive the best price on your transaction.

You are the one most likely able to provide your family the knowledge that will be essential to the furtherance of your collection.

CHAPTER 6

For the Coin Collector: Knowledge of Importance to Your Family

We have already addressed the need to provide detailed guidance to your heirs regarding disposition of your collection. It is also important to provide your heirs with some basic knowledge about coin collecting to properly prepare them to preserve and protect the coins.

Having handled coins for many years, you may assume some things to be obvious when they are not so to the average person.

For example, no collector would take a scouring pad and rub the surface of a coin to produce a nice shine. However, time and time again, I have encountered the family member whose first action in collecting is to clean the coins they've inherited. Proper care of coins and other numismatic knowledge is best transmitted while you are alive, so that questions can be answered. Obviously, a clear part of your instructions should guide your family on preserving and protecting your collection.

You might have placed some of your coins in temporary plastic inserts containing some PVC, planning to remove them long before they would suffer chemical damage. But if you don't communicate your intentions and the dangers of leaving coins in such containers, that information might be lost to your family. You should provide clear guidance to your family with regard to:

- **Security.** Identify what coins are of sufficient value that they should be kept in a bank safety deposit box.
- **Location.** Detail where your collection is located and explain if any of it is hidden (often you hear a story of someone who purchases a house and finds coins in a wall during remodeling).
- **Insurance.** Record which (if any) parts of your collection are insured and include the details of the coverage.
- **Preservation.** Provide instructions on storage and handling.

Special Section: Environmental Damage

People inexperienced with coin collecting are not likely to understand how coins may become damaged as a result of improper storage and/or handling.

Most coin collectors are familiar with the common inexpensive flexible plastic container referred to as a "PVC flip," which consists of two pockets, one for a coin and the other for an informational card. These packets, typically just slightly smaller than two inches square, often contain polyvinyl chloride, or PVC. This compound may react with the surface of a coin and greatly detract from its appearance. The most common effect of the PVC reaction is the formation of a greenish, slimy substance on the surface of a silver coin.

Note that moisture increases the rate of chemical reactions that can alter the surface of a coin. It is very important to store coins in an environment where an appropriate humidity level is maintained.

There are also some coin album pages made of a certain paper that contains chemicals that can react with the surface of a coin. It is very important that higher-value coins be stored in containers which will not react with the coin surface over a long period of time.

The PVC used in these popular "flips" can damage the surface of your coins. Note that not every coin flip contains PVC.

SECURITY

Coins are often the target of thieves, as they can usually be easily sold (with the exceptions of certain very scarce identifiable items), especially if the seller is not concerned with obtaining fair value. It is important that your family understands how to protect a collection from theft and takes appropriate actions to protect it.

Security starts with privacy; if thieves are unaware of your collection, it will not become a likely target. Many collectors take steps intended to preserve the privacy of their interests. For example, don't have coin magazines and/or publications delivered to your home. Many collectors use post office boxes as one means of protecting their anonymity.

A concern today is the use of social media. For example, it is probably not a good idea to post to Facebook, Twitter, or an open forum that you just acquired a coin collection. A general guideline would be to not mention or advertise your collection to anyone other than those who "need to know"—for example, people with whom you are attempting to make transactions. In those instances where you do need to discuss your collection, try to avoid mention of your address or other personal data so that you minimize the likelihood that such information falls into the wrong hands.

When carrying your coins to show them for sale, take some care not to become a target of a thief. For example, taking expensive coins around the tables at a coin show might identify you as a target to thieves who frequent these venues. Be aware of your surroundings and stay alert.

PRESERVATION

Preservation of your coins is also important to assure that their value is not diminished by improper handling or storage. This is most important for higher-value and higher-condition coins. Your family should understand the proper way to hold and view coins and also be aware that their surfaces should never be manipulated by amateurs, whatever the intent. Cleaning a coin might make it appear more attractive to an amateur, but it greatly reduces its value in the marketplace. If your collection is being liquidated quickly, the concerns of improper storage may not be as significant, but for those portions of the collection which are to be retained, it is important to understand those methods which will prevent the occurrence of unattractive toning and/or other forms of surface damage to your coin.

Some posit that cleaning coins with soap and water or olive oil will not damage the coins and can restore them to a more attractive appearance. You should inform your heirs, however, that no method of coin cleaning is guaranteed to achieve good results and is therefore best left undone.

- - - - -

INSURANCE

Most homeowner insurance policies provide little or no coverage for coins or other collectibles. Therefore, if you need to protect yourself while you are holding the coins, you may want to consider the purchase of a policy available directly from companies that specialize in insuring collectibles. Alternatively, you might decide to place your most valuable coins in safety deposit boxes and rely on bank security.

LOCATION

If you have a large coin collection, it is likely that it is stored in several places, perhaps with very different security profiles. You might have your most valuable pieces stored in a bank safety deposit box or a well-designed hidden area in your home. Common or lower-value items may be stored in more visible locations. It is important that your heirs know where to find the entire collection, and it is usually best if you walk them through these locations as a part of your preparation. You don't want them to fail to benefit from the value of coins that might be carefully hidden in places so secret that even your family could not find them.

For coins of certain value, security measures such as the use of safety deposit boxes might be prudent. Should you take this step, make sure to inform your heirs and provide them with access to your boxes at the appropriate time.

• • • • •

If portions of your collection are hidden in secure areas of your home, make sure to instruct your heirs on how to find these spots.

*Delaying the decisions on how to prepare
your collection for its eventual disposition
is the surest way to diminish its value.*

CHAPTER 7

For the Coin Collector: Preparing Your Collection for Your Heirs

Like many coin collectors, you have probably invested a substantial amount of your time, as well as the financial resources of your family, in pursuit of your collecting interests. You have done so both for personal enjoyment and also with the hope of building value which will ultimately benefit your family. Unfortunately, it is not likely that you have taken the time to prepare your collection for ultimate transfer to family members and, as a result, the desired financial benefits may not be realized. Unprepared family members may not be able to handle your collection, and it may needlessly add to their burden at an inconvenient time. Insufficient preparation may also add tensions to the probate process, resulting in conflicts among your heirs should they differ on how they would like your collection to be allocated.

Coin collecting is a very complex hobby, and also a very expensive one. Even collectors with modest collecting budgets often build collections worth tens or hundreds of thousands of dollars over many decades. Most collectors primarily purchase or accumulate coins and do not develop much expertise in selling coins at fair value.

Your coin collection likely contains many coins (hundreds or thousands), some of which are worth a lot of money individually and many more that are of lower value. Some portions of your collection may have greater sentimental or emotional value due to their origin, method of acquisition, or personal significance. Other portions may have no particular importance and may have been randomly accumulated over many years.

Typically, the organization of the collection is variable, with some portions quite nicely cataloged and graded and others awaiting your attention. Very few collectors completely catalog their entire collection in a comprehensive manner. This lack of organization, if not resolved by you prior to your death, greatly increases the difficulty of handling the disposition of the collection in the future.

Organizing both your collection and your thoughts on its disposition or preservation will help your heirs make the most of their inheritance.

◆ ◆ ◆ ◆ ◆

Unfortunately, if your collection is not prepared for the transfer to your family members, the end result is an unplanned-for acquisition of a collection by family members who are completely unprepared to handle it.

There are several major considerations which will be addressed in the remaining chapters of this section:

- Consolidating your collection for disposition
- Dividing your collection among your heirs
- Documenting what you know about the grades and values of your coins
- Documenting your recommendations on selling strategies
- Providing a list of recommended contacts to assist your heirs with disposition
- Identifying portions of the collection with heirloom value which you would like kept in the family if possible

There is much you can do to reduce the burden on your heirs. You have detailed knowledge of all facets of the collection and usually understand how coins were acquired. You may have established relationships with others involved in buying and selling coins. You might have direct experience with some sales transactions.

Of equal importance is that you know the current state of the collection. This includes where most of the value is concentrated, what items

are cataloged and graded, what items are adequately stored and protected, and many other facets. When your heir receives a collection without the benefit of this knowledge, it is easy for them to make mistakes
that result in a reduction of the value of the collection. These mistakes
could range from failing to remove coins from temporary coin holders
to improperly cleaning or handling coins. Heirs might also sell coins at
much less than their achievable market value should they lack sufficient
information.

You know the circumstances of your heirs and are therefore best positioned to allocate the collection fairly and in a manner most likely to provide optimal benefit to your family. You can also use the allocation process
to influence what parts of your collection remain within the family.

During your years of collecting, you have probably come in contact with
a variety of people involved in the hobby. You may have purchased coins
from many different sources, and you likely have strong opinions as to
which people you would like to do business with as well as people you
would not recommend. You may have had contact with other collectors
or perhaps joined a local coin club.

It is possible that you have considered sales of some of your coins or
even consummated some transactions. Any such experience should be
captured and passed along to your heirs.

Most collectors constantly postpone the tasks of organizing their collection for their heirs, and the end result is that it never happens due to
infirmity or death. The time to organize your collection is now, not later.
Even if you have many more years of collecting ahead, efforts to simplify
your collection will probably enhance your enjoyment of the hobby as
well as your attainment of high-interest collecting objectives. You should
view this effort as a new dimension to the hobby of coin collecting. You
should approach it with excitement as you seek to receive fair value as
you sell parts of your collection, all the while knowing you are helping
your family and also freeing up funds for further pursuit of collecting or
other family needs.

As you fully engage in simplifying your collection, you are likely to connect with new individuals engaged in coin collecting and explore many
new facets of the hobby. The remaining chapters of this section should
provide you with a road map for the disposition of your collection and
encouragement so that you can overcome the inertia that leads to inaction. Hopefully, presented with the reality of the decisions you face, you
will be able to make trade-offs that make sense in your particular circumstance and progress rapidly towards simplification of your collection.

Collections received by heirs without proper consideration and preparation are least likely to survive or provide the benefits intended by the collector.

CHAPTER 8

For the Coin Collector: Allocation to Your Heirs

Depending on the composition of your family, you may have one heir who will inherit your entire collection or a number of heirs for which you will need to divide the collection equitably. Your immediate heir might be your spouse, but you might wish to allocate part of your collection for eventual disposition to a number of children or grandchildren. There may also be interest among your extended family or friends that you wish to consider in your planning.

There are many considerations with respect to the disposition of your collection. Your heirs will likely have different degrees of interest in coin collecting, and they'll also have different financial needs. One child might wish to retain and grow your collection, whereas another might plan to immediately liquidate and use the cash generated for other purposes. This interest should be a primary consideration in how you allocate your collection.

If your immediate heirs have no interest in coin collecting and would liquidate any coins that they inherit, consider that you may have extended family or friends with interest in coin collecting who would like to acquire all or part of your collection. By planning for disposition of your collection while you are able to do so, you will be able to devise the strategy most likely to produce the optimal result.

There are several situations you may encounter in the allocation process and a variety of strategies for planning the disposition of your collection. The best strategy will account for the situations and interest of your descendants as well as the importance you place on continuation of some of the collection. This section examines some of the most common family situations and discusses strategies that might be used effectively.

Situation 1: None of your heirs has any interest in maintaining the collection. This is one of the most commonly encountered situations. Coin collecting is a hobby lacking the participation of many young people, probably in part due to the difficulty of finding old coins in circulation and the expense associated with purchasing them. You are probably in a very good position to judge the interest among your heirs. If you have not seen or nurtured any coin-collecting interest in them while you are alive, it is unlikely that the interest really exists.

If this is your situation, there are two basic strategies that can make sense, as well as some variations. One strategy is to liquidate your collection, increasing the cash value of your estate. The benefit of this approach is that, as a result of your experience with coin collecting, you are likely to sell your collection with far more favorable results than those that might be achieved by unknowledgeable family members. This will provide your family with the maximum financial benefit from your years of collecting and also completely eliminate the burden they would face in liquidating the collection later. The downside of this strategy is that you may prematurely sell your collection and not benefit from your continued enjoyment of the hobby for a number of years.

A different approach at the alternate end of the spectrum is to continue working on your entire collection and make an allocation to your heirs based on equal value, expecting they will liquidate it shortly after acquisi-

In the instance that none of your heirs will want to preserve your collection, you'll need to weigh the option of selling your collection now versus that of leaving the task to your heirs.

tion. This allows you to continue your collecting interest but likely diminishes the ultimate value to be received by your heirs, and it places the entire burden of the sales effort on them.

I believe that the best strategy is one that combines the two strategies above, balancing the current interest of the collector against the future interests of your heirs. I would recommend selling as much of the collection as possible, retaining that part which most greatly contributes to your enjoyment. In this way you do not have to eliminate your enjoyment completely, and at the same time you achieve a better value on that part of the collection that is sold. Also, with your simplified collection, you may be able to provide more detailed guidance to your heirs, enabling them to achieve better results on the part of the collection they sell. Any coins that are sold will also reduce the burden on your family.

Situation 1A: None of your heirs has any interest in coin collecting, but there are members of your extended family and/or close friends who would like to acquire parts of your collection. The interested parties would not normally be included as a part of your estate planning, so any portions of the collection they receive might affect the ultimate proceeds received by your heirs. There are several variations to this situation, each which can be addressed in different ways.

- **Disposition to a close friend.** You may have a close friend who would like to acquire portions of your collection. You may have specific items he is missing that would enable him to complete his collection. Perhaps you have worked together in pursuit of your collections and his interest in some aspects of your collection were developed as a result. A simple solution exists if your friend is able to afford purchase of the items at fair market value and is willing to do so. In this case, sale of these items to your friend both meets his needs and also simplifies the liquidation of your collection for your heirs.

  One issue is whether to consummate the sale while you are still collecting or to make it effective upon your death. If you sell the item to your friend immediately, you establish a fair price, your friend receives the coin, and you receive a check. The proceeds then increase your assets and will grow in value over time. The downside is that the coins you sell no longer contribute to your collecting pursuits.

  Alternately, you could provide a direction to your heirs that the coins be sold to your friend upon your death. The problem with this approach is that the fair market value may have changed, and of

Disposition of your collection to a close friend can give you both a solid return as well as the satisfaction of knowing that your coins will be retained and appreciated.

* * * * *

course, the economic circumstances of your friend may be different. Your friend may no longer be interested in collecting, or he may have acquired the item by other means. A deferred arrangement greatly increases the complexity of the transaction and increases the likelihood of bad feelings between your friend and surviving family. Though this approach enables you to maintain the coin as a part of your collection, it is at a great potential cost.

Based on these considerations, the best practical approach if you wish a friend to receive part of your collection is to consummate this transaction while you are alive. This enables you to determine the price at which the transaction will occur. You might choose to sell the coin at below fair market value to your friend, and you clearly can do so if you wish. Though the coin will no longer be a part of your collection, you will certainly feel a great sense of gratification in that you have helped a friend and the coin will remain in good hands. Meanwhile, you can undoubtedly find other aspects of your collection to pursue.

One other consideration would be the willingness of your friend to allow you to retain possession of the coin while you are alive for your continued enjoyment. Though this might make you feel more comfortable with the sale, it again creates a potential future problem if for some reason your heirs do not acknowledge your friend's ownership of the coin or try to contest it due to the amount of value it holds.

The bottom line here is that you really don't want to receive a small benefit of collecting enjoyment if it could ultimately produce strife among your friends and family. Keep things simple and complete the transaction fully while you have control over your collection.

• **Disposition to an extended family member.** You might have other family members (cousins, nieces, nephews, et al.) who would not normally be included in your estate but do have a strong interest in coin collecting. For this reason, you may wish to break tradition and include them in your planning, but your ability to do so will be impacted by the financial circumstances of all involved. Perhaps your estate has sufficient value to meet the needs of your immediate family and the amount of value in your collection you wish to give to extended family members is small by comparison. In this circumstance, you can either gift the items to your relatives while alive or specifically include them in your will. In this case, the simple approach of gifting them while you are in control is still best. Including them as a part of your estate introduces several issues.

For example, all parties included in your estate are entitled to understand the full accounting of the will and also to be given status requiring notification of proceedings relevant to the will. You may not wish your extended family members to have detailed knowledge of your assets or estate, but including them in your will may result in this unintended consequence. It also gives them awareness and status with respect to probate, and as a result they might choose to contest the will based on other assets with which you did not intend for them to be involved. For example, perhaps there was some family property that you acquired at a very low value to which some of the extended family members felt they had a claim. The best way to avoid these complexities is to gift the items while you are alive and thus totally avoid inclusion of additional parties in your probate proceedings.

Probate is complicated enough and often managed by an inexperienced executor who may be an inheritor. You do not want to complicate your heirs' challenge by involving other parties who would otherwise not need to be included.

It is also possible that the items you would like to leave to your extended family members hold too much value to just gift. They might represent too great a portion of your estate, and therefore you may feel that it is necessary that they be transacted in a way to compensate your estate for their loss. This situation is further complicated by the financial circumstances of the intended recipient and whether or not they can afford to purchase the items. If your family member can afford but does not wish to purchase the items, the choice is easy, and there is no reason for further consideration. The items should be sold at fair market value to a disinterested third party and the proceeds added to your assets. After all, if your family member does not choose to purchase the items, there is no reason for you to gift them at the expense of your heirs.

On the other hand, if your family member cannot afford the purchase, you will still likely need to sell the items at fair market value and use the proceeds to increase your assets. You may, however, be able to separate some lower-value portions which you can gift to this heir without greatly diminishing your estate. In this way, you have aided your family member and at the same time preserved most of the value of your estate.

Involving an extended family member such as a nephew can complicate the probate process, but this option may offer the opportunity of both maintaining the collection and satisfying your immediate heirs' needs.

♦ **Donation to a museum or other third party.** When you have no interested family members and know that your coins will be liquidated by your heirs, it is possible that there are pieces you would like to donate to a museum of other party for public display. This is clearly your prerogative. Quite simply, if you are comfortable with the estate assets that you will leave to your heirs without receiving fair market value for certain pieces, you can dispose of those items any way you want. This should be done while you are in full control of your collection and as soon as you decide you are sure that is what you want to do. You could, of course, also include these as a part of your estate, but that also introduces additional complexity to your probate process and has many of the same potential problems as including other family members.

Situation 1B: None of your direct heirs has any interest in coin collecting, but you have interested family members who would be indirectly provided for in your estate. There are several variations of this situation. It most often arises when the collector has an interested grandchild whose parent has no interest in coin collecting or has greater financial needs. Depending on the specifics, there are several approaches.

Passing some of your coins on to a grandchild serves a dual purpose: preserving a portion of your collection and fostering interest in numismatics among youth.

If the dollar amount involved is not great, you might be able to gift a portion of your collection to an interested grandchild and at the same time gift comparable financial assets to other grandchildren so the distribution is equitable.

If the dollar amount is large, gifting it to a grandchild might require reduction of the financial assets gifted to his parents. This can be a more difficult situation and is best resolved through discussions between the interested parties.

Situation 2: One of your heirs wishes to continue your collection, and the others do not. Your interest in coin collecting may have resulted in one of your heirs becoming interested as well. In this situation, you would like to be able to keep intact the most important portions of your collection by passing them on to the interested heir. Most likely, however, you will want to equitably compensate other heirs so that your estate is distributed in the portions you consider fair. This is complicated by likely differences in the financial situations of you and/or your heirs.

The simplest case is when your estate has sufficient financial assets so that you can pass along the entire collection, intact, to your interested heir and then increase the financial assets for the remaining heirs to compensate. With this strategy, the primary challenge is to set a fair value on the coin collection. Most collectors and value guides provide valuations based on replacement cost. This is of interest for insurance purposes, but for the purposes of allocating fair value to heirs, calculating the current value which would be received from a sale of the coins would be the more accurate method of evaluation. Of course, this figure is more difficult to estimate, as the sales value is dependent on many variables, including how the coins will be sold, transaction costs, the effort required for the sale, and the market demand for the individual items.

A further complexity of assigning value to the coins is the timing of the valuation. Coin market values are volatile and change with time. If you leave this valuation to your executor, it may create many problems. The executor could be the family member who is to inherit the coins or another family member who is to receive compensating proceeds. Either situation produces a clear conflict of interest. At the same time, assigning the value immediately is also problematic in that the value may change substantially between your allocation and the inheritance, potentially resulting in greatly uneven outcomes in either direction.

There are several ways to avoid these problems. You might determine that the valuation is to be set at the time of the actual transfer based upon

If you have just one heir who would be interested in preserving your collection, take the time to consider the timing of any valuation of your coins and how that factors into your allocation.

✦ ✦ ✦ ✦ ✦

a specific price guide, with a defined adjustment factor. For example, items with numismatic value might be set at 80% of Red Book prices while items valued for bullion are set at 90% of spot price for silver and 95% for gold. These valuations are not perfect and will likely produce some inequities, but they at least remove the conflicts of interest that would otherwise occur.

A second approach would be to assign the value now and take an equivalent amount of money and invest it conservatively in a separate investment which is allocated proportionately to the remaining heirs. In this way, both the recipient of your collection and your other heirs will see value fluctuation based on the assets' performance during the period between the assignment and probate. Of course, this also can produce an uneven result, but at least the reason can be explained and is defensible.

You might wish to avoid these potential inequities and other problems totally. One way this can be accomplished is to gift the coins now and gift your other heirs equivalent value at the same time in cash. Each heir can then decide how to handle their gift, and there will be no impact on a future probate proceeding. If one heir decides to invest their gift in the stock market and triples it and another spends it on a new car, those are choices they make for themselves. Of course, in order to take this approach you need to be sure that your needs and those of your spouse are already met.

The recommended approach is a valuation applying a discount percentage based on the nature of the asset. Below are some general guidelines which can be adjusted for your particular knowledge and selling experience.

- **Rare or scarce items of high value.** Such items offer the opportunity to use those sales methods likely to achieve the best return (major auction and/or dealer consignment). These items often are sold above retail value, and therefore you should value these pieces at 100% of retail price.

- **Mid-range, easily replaceable coins in the range of $50 to $1,900 each.** Avenues available for sale of these coins range from outright sale to a dealer to sale through daily certified-coin auctions. You might use a starting estimate of 70% of retail price.

- **Coins worth bullion value.** It is easy to sell coins with bullion content. The best results will be achieved when dealing directly with a refiner, as any middleman will take a profit. Sales at retail stores usually return very poor results. Mail-order dealers advertise their bullion prices, usually deal directly with a refiner, and handle a high enough volume to be competitive. As a rule of thumb, estimate 90% of the spot price for gold and 80% of the spot price for silver when dealing with small quantities (up to 10 ounces for gold and up to 100 ounces for silver). Selling larger quantities might enable you to receive as much as 98% of spot price for gold and 90% of spot price or better for silver.

    When making such valuations, keep in mind that your calculation must take account of the actual precious-metal content. Ingots, for example, are typically manufactured to a high degree of purity (fineness)—perhaps .9999 or .99999—resulting in essentially pure precious-metal content equivalent to the actual weight. Coins, on the other hand, are often manufactured at varying purities, resulting in precious-metal content that is less than the overall coin weight. When calculating bullion content, the fineness must be multiplied by the coin weight to determine the bullion weight; both of the necessary figures for these calculations are provided in coin guides such as the Red Book. Also, for older coins with considerable wear, the actual weight can be substantially less than the specified weight of a new coin. Again, the refiner is only going to pay for the actual precious metal they receive.

✦ **Low-value coins.** Low-value coins are difficult to sell near retail values due to the transaction costs involved. For example, suppose you have 50 Eisenhower dollars with a total retail value of $100. You can turn these in at the bank for face value and receive $50 with essentially no transaction cost if you do it while conducting other business. Suppose, however, a dealer is offering to buy these at 70% of retail ($70). You will then need to insure and mail them and/or drive somewhere. You will likely spend $10 in either instance and thereby only gain $10 more than turning them in at the bank. If you also factor in the value of your time, it is likely that you receive no real benefit.

A realistic way to value such items is at slightly higher than face value (perhaps 10% more) or at an actual bulk purchase price you can find in the wanted section of a weekly coin newspaper (less $10 for mailing and insurance).

These are intended as guidelines, as your situation may be different as a result of your geographical proximity to coin dealers and your experiences in selling coins. But in lieu of greater knowledge on your part, these would probably produce a fairer allocation to your heirs than an allocation based on retail value.

Situation 2A: One of your heirs wishes to continue your collection and the others do not, but financial realities don't allow disposition of the entire collection to the interested heir. This situation can occur when you do not have enough financial assets to compensate your other heirs for the value of the collection should it be given to the interested heir. A similar scenario also arises if the interested heir's financial situation is such that other needs don't justify maintaining so much money tied up in a coin collection. There are many variations to this situation, but the overriding goal is the same. You will want to provide sufficient financial resources to each of your heirs (consistent with your own desire to do so),

Clear communication of financial realities will be important
in the allocation process.

* * * * *

distribute your assets equitably (as per your own definition), and optimize that portion of your collection that remains in the family.

Whatever the reason, the solution is the same. Basically, a sufficient portion of the collection must be sold so that the end result is an affordable
collection for the interested heir and compensating financial assets for
the others. In this circumstance, it is best that the coins to be sold are sold
by the collector, so that highest value can be achieved and the smallest
portion of the coins sold. Leaving this challenge to the heirs would not
only likely diminish the value received but could result in conflict and
disagreement due to the various pressures that could emerge.

It is likely that you will need to consult with your heirs during the process of this planning. With regard to the heir who is to receive a portion
of your collection, it is really best to let them decide how much of your
collection they would like to receive, understanding that it will result in

the reduction of the financial assets they receive. Only your heirs can decide what is best for them. This discussion may be further complicated by their marital situation. Their spouse might not share their interest in coin collecting and could view money spent on their hobby as detracting from other family needs. In that case, introduction of a decision involving a substantial amount of money may bring with it marital strife. Obviously, that is not something you want to create. If you believe the possibility exists that starting such a discussion could cause problems for your heir, avoid the issue entirely and gift less-valuable portions to this heir outright. If you are unsure, be very attentive after starting the dialog for any hint of a problem, and if such signs emerge, back away from the process quickly.

If such problems do not exist, you and your heir can work together to decide what portions of the collection will be inherited or transferred and what financial value will be provided to other heirs to effect a balance. This is the best way to assure a result that meets everyone's needs and will be well received.

Situation 3: You have several interested heirs. This situation resembles Situation 2 in that it requires a division of the coin collection itself among the heirs, and it also involves some of the same financial issues that need to be resolved in Situation 2. The division of the collection would best be done jointly by you and your interested heirs based on interest in particular portions of the collection. Once the collection itself is divided, the financial realities and your desire to treat all heirs equitably may then be applied and, if necessary, portions of your coins sold. Again, this allocation is best determined through group discussions so that the end result satisfies everyone.

As a guiding rule in these situations, start with the assumption that preservation of the collection is not worth family strife. If you know that opening a dialog on more complicated distributions would cause such strife, do not do so. If, on the other hand, you believe an accommodation is likely, the issue should be cautiously approached, and in the event unexpected issues arise, abandoned quickly.

SPECIAL SECTION: GIFTING PORTIONS OF YOUR COLLECTION WHILE YOU ARE ALIVE

If you have one or more interested heirs and have determined a fair formula for allocating your assets among your heirs, you might find it advantageous to gift some portions of your collection while you are living. You might transfer ownership but agree that you will keep possession of the coins while you are alive. Any acquisitions or sales affecting that part of the collection would be done by the new owner, but you would continue to enjoy those portions of the collection, buoyed by the likelihood that these coins will remain in your family for many years to come due to your planning.

Gifting a portion of your collection while alive can make the allocation process (not to mention the gift shopping process) easier.

CLOSING POINTS

Obviously, the specific situations outlined in this work represent only a sample of the situations you might encounter. Other specific scenarios you face can be addressed by combining some or all of the above approaches. The key to a successful outcome is keeping in mind the fundamental goals and parameters that likely exist in all scenarios:

- Optimal retention in your family of items of special significance to you
- Fair treatment of all family members, using whatever parameters you consider appropriate to define "fair"
- Avoidance of conflict and/or strife among your family members and friends as a result of how you choose to allocate your collection
- Simplification of the challenges faced by your executor at the time of probate
- Elimination of the need for your heirs to be involved in selling coins without the knowledge or interest to do so in a successful manner
- Avoidance of the introduction of nonessential parties to the probate proceeding
- Avoidance of financial loss through estate taxation by transferring assets while you are alive
- Satisfaction of the collecting interests of your heirs, extended family members, and friends to the extent such can be attained
- Preservation of your own enjoyment of your collection for as long as possible
- Avoidance of liquidation of your collection at poor value (whenever it might occur)
- Reciprocation to the coin-collecting hobby as a return for your enjoyment of the hobby over many years

Consideration of the above as each point relates to whatever decisions you make increases the likelihood of a successful disposition.

To summarize: You have invested a substantial amount of time and money in collecting over the years and generally would want your heirs to receive maximum benefits from your pursuits. You also would not want your collection to result in family conflict. It is clear, therefore, that it is you who are in the best position to achieve the best possible results with appropriate planning and partial dispositions where needed.

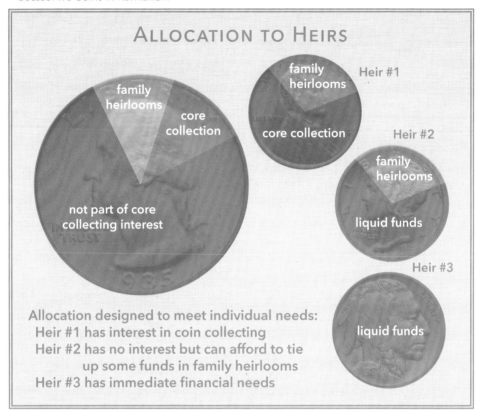

ALLOCATION TO HEIRS

family heirlooms

core collection

not part of core collecting interest

1935

Heir #1

family heirlooms

core collection

Heir #2

family heirlooms

liquid funds

Heir #3

liquid funds

Allocation designed to meet individual needs:
Heir #1 has interest in coin collecting
Heir #2 has no interest but can afford to tie
up some funds in family heirlooms
Heir #3 has immediate financial needs

These charts show how one might allocate assets to three heirs, one of whom has interest in coin collecting, one of whom is not interested in coin collecting but can afford to inherit some heirlooms in place of liquid funds, and one of whom is best served inheriting only liquid funds.

CASE STUDY: SAMPLE CONSOLIDATION OF A COLLECTION

John had been collecting coins since he was a child, initially pulling coins from circulation. He started collecting in the late 1930s, mainly Indian Head and Lincoln (Wheat Ears Reverse) cents, Buffalo nickels, Mercury dimes, and Washington quarters. As the years passed, John's attention turned to family and career, but his interest in coin collecting persisted and as time permitted he added to his collection.

Later in his career, personal finances allowed John to invest more in coin collecting and, as a result of his special interest in the aforementioned series, he focused his expenditures on obtaining complete sets of these coins in MS-64 condition. By the time he reached retirement, he had completed these sets with the exception of a few key dates in each. A couple decades prior to his retirement the American Silver Eagles were issued, and he also began to collect a full set of these coins.

All told, John's entire collection totaled almost 10,000 coins. Many were low-grade examples pulled from circulation. Several hundred others were a part of his core coin collection. None of John's coins were professionally certified, as he had no plans to sell any coins, and most of them were purchased before the advent of third-party certification—except for the recent purchases, which he bought directly from the U.S. Mint.

John's collection occupied several safety deposit boxes as well as a number of containers at his home. Security was an ongoing concern, and John realized his insurance coverage would not replace his collection in the event of theft or fire.

None of John's children shared his interest in coin collecting. Some of them were in excellent financial circumstances, and others were struggling. Coin collecting was one of John's happiest pursuits, and he wished to continue in retirement. However, he recognized that if he were to become seriously ill or pass away, his family would struggle with his collection and most likely sell it at a value far less than its worth.

John started by making a list of his collecting interests and ranked them based on their significance and contribution to his enjoyment. He had an inventory of his collection, which he had recently updated. He also thought carefully of how much money was tied up in his collection and how he would like to change this in the coming years.

After a careful review, John decided on the collecting objectives he would like to pursue. These included:

- completion of his Mercury dime and Buffalo nickel collection,
- completion of a new collection of Peace dollars,
- completion and continuation of his collection of American Silver Eagles.

John decided that the remainder of his collection had really provided most of the enjoyment it was going to and that he would attempt to sell it at fair value and continue to receive enjoyment from this process. He decided he would handle the sales process first and then divide the proceeds. Part of the proceeds would be used to continue his collecting, and the remainder would increase the financial assets of his family.

John started by studying a number of different approaches to selling coins. He also began to monitor online auction Web sites to learn what coins were appropriate for these sales venues and what returns could be expected. Based on this education, John decided to start by mailing a number of his higher-value coins to a professional online auction service. His selection of coins for the auction was based on his monitoring of prices realized for similar coins. While John waited for the first auction of his coins, he separated out all of the coins he owned that were worth bullion value. He then contacted several dealers and sold these coins to a reputable firm that offered both the price closest to the current spot value and also quick payment.

About six weeks later, John received his first check from the initial auction and determined he was satisfied with the result. He then began periodic shipments to the auction house for the additional coins he wished to sell. John was not in a great rush, so he decided he would take a year to perform this process.

At this point, remaining in John's collection were an assortment of items including modern government-issued Mint and Proof sets, bags of low-grade cents and nickels from which key dates had been removed, rolls of Brilliant Uncirculated coins from the 1960s, and a few key coins of higher value that he had obtained during the years he collected.

He decided that his interest in the rolls of Brilliant Uncirculated pieces, bulk coins, and government sets was not high and

John took the time to crystallize his thoughts and put pen to paper regarding his collecting priorities, and this gave him direction heading forward into both disposition of less important pieces and acquisition of coins that he truly wanted.

✦ ✦ ✦ ✦ ✦

that he would not spend much time working with them. He mailed many of these to dealers for immediate sale in response to buy ads in numismatic papers. Some of the coins were not worth mailing, and he decided to return them to circulation for other new collectors to find.

The few high-value coins were not certified and, depending on their actual grade, had the potential to be very valuable. He had 15 such coins and decided to spend several hundred dollars to have them certified. The results were very good, as the total Greysheet valuation for all the coins amounted to about $60,000 based on the grades assigned, and the *Coin World* retail valuation amounted to $90,000. John lived in a city with several local coin dealers, one of whom he knew very well. He decided to consign the graded pieces to the dealer for sale. The terms included an agreed-upon commission and an incentive to obtain a higher price. John realized $88,000 from the sale of these coins, with some selling at prices slightly higher than Greysheet values but also a few scarcer coins at higher than *Coin World* retail prices.

After a year, John's efforts realized about $100,000 in cash, and his collection was reduced to the Mercury dimes, Buffalo nickels, and American Silver Eagles, as well as a few other pieces in a box that he decided to keep. He had greatly diminished the bulk of his collection. As a result of the experience he had gained, he understood the true value of the coins he kept and would also be a smarter buyer in his future purchases. John decided to allocate 2/3 of his proceeds ($67,000) to increase his financial assets and 1/3 ($33,000) to his remaining collecting objectives. This would include the continuation of purchases of Silver Eagles, as well as key dates in the series on which he focused.

Missing in his Silver Eagle collection was the 1995-W (the series key) and one of the Reverse Proofs. He decided to allocate $4,000 to purchase these items. Missing from the Mercury dime collection was the 1916-D and the 1942, 2 Over 1. There were also several coins in his collection he wanted to replace with higher-grade examples. Missing from his Buffalo nickel collection were two key dates. The Peace dollar collection would be a new effort. He decided to allocate about $15,000 to the Peace dollar collection and the remainder to enhancement and completion of the Buffalo nickel and Mercury dime collections.

Based on what he had learned over the past year and using the proceeds of his sales, he could now set realistic collecting objectives based on available funds and his knowledge of the market.

John met with his children to discuss what he had accomplished and what would happen to the remainder of his collection. During this meeting, none of his children expressed interest in continuing the collection, but one (who was in excellent financial shape) indicated that he recognized the significance of the remainder of the collection and that he would retain it if at all possible. Thus, John decided that the collection should be left to that child and that the other children should be provided with offsetting financial assets based on a realistic sales valuation of the collection. John also provided to his son who would inherit the coins a detailed explanation of how to determine the worth of the collection when it came time to sell, as well as a recommended sales strategy.

As a result of John's efforts, he had spent much enjoyable time in the process of selling parts of his collection, all the while knowing that he was greatly simplifying the burden on his family. He was also very pleased to know that his family would receive fair value for his efforts. And finally, he had become much more knowledgeable about coin collecting and realized his approach to acquiring coins to complete his collections would be very different.

After several years of effort, John neared completion of the objectives he set. He had a small amount of money remaining to invest in the hobby. He continued his efforts to enhance his core collections by upgrading individual coins to more attractive specimens. Armed with very specific needs, he attended local coin shows and met with other collectors and dealers to locate the special items he sought. He also continued to purchase a small number of other items that did not fit his collecting strategy but provided enjoyment at low cost.

When John ultimately passed, his collection was inherited by the son who had agreed to retain it, and his other children received the corresponding cash which would provide them with some needed financial security. The remainder of the collection was never sold, as the son who inherited kept it as a family heirloom. The collection did not occupy much space, could easily be kept safe, and—as a result of John's efforts after retirement—was constituted so as to retain and increase in value over the years.

John took time to pursue the last few coins missing from his specialized collections with the funds earned from disposition of other pieces in which he was less interested.

SECTION II

For Inheritors

Section II addresses the issues faced by the inheritor. It provides a general discussion of all important areas—divided into a series of stages—with guidance on where to gain additional knowledge.

As an heir, formulating a deliberate strategy and incorporating any guidance provided by the collector will result in generally best enable you to evaluate, preserve, or sell a coin collection.

CHAPTER 9

For the Inheritor: Issues Involved in Managing an Inherited Collection

For someone without coin-collecting experience, the task of managing the disposition of an inherited collection can be daunting. Trying to obtain fair value for hard assets that you do not understand is both stressful and likely to produce poor results. Many inheritors do not know where to start and are completely overwhelmed. As a result, many sell the collection quickly for cash, but this method frequently returns only a small portion of the potential value of the collection.

The goal of this section is to remove the mystery surrounding a coin collection and lay out the basic issues that need to be understood. It also offers recommendations for how to approach the task in a methodological manner, making it less likely that you feel overwhelmed. Knowledge of the process of selling coins is your best friend in managing the liquidation of a collection. A few weeks of time spent on research will result in substantially better returns during the actual sale and will also provide you with the confidence needed to receive fair value.

No matter the situation, the most important starting point is an accurate inventory of your collection. This will be necessary to adequately insure it against loss and also to determine a disposition strategy. If you are fortunate, the collector will have cataloged a substantial portion of their collection in either software designed for this purpose or some sort of hand-written log. Either represents a good starting point for your inventory. If the catalog was done by hand, browse the written lists and identify those coins marked as having the highest value. Then attempt to locate these coins and confirm that the inventory description is aligned with the actual coin with respect to type, grade, etc.

If the collector maintained an inventory in a program designed for this purpose, it will probably be necessary for you to learn to use this tool. Though some upfront learning may be required, this time will be very well spent, as these tools are likely to greatly assist you during the sales process. If necessary, contact the software vendor for assistance. Since most numismatic software publishers are small businesses, you may find that the software vendors can provide you with assistance in getting started and also some general guidance on how to proceed.

Taking a step back to learn about your inherited collection and evaluate your disposition options will result in better returns.

❖ ❖ ❖ ❖ ❖

If the collector did not take the time to inventory the collection, or substantial parts were not cataloged, it will be up to you to make this inventory. You may find it useful to acquire software intended for this purpose that can ease your efforts. Some software products are available that can assist you in understanding the process of buying and selling coins, as well as provide assistance in grading coins in the event that portions of the collection have not been graded. The book *Cash In Your Coins: Selling the Rare Coins You've Inherited,* by Beth Deisher, has an illustrated chapter on identifying coin types. The annually issued Red Book also has photographs of every U.S. coin type minted since the 1700s.

When you get started, it is important to understand that a large collection is complicated and that you cannot organize, inventory, and sell it all at once. You therefore must focus your attention on those items of greatest value and/or interest. It is possible that, as you proceed, you decide that the undertaking is one that you do not want to pursue to the end. By addressing the most valuable items first, you are most likely to at least address the areas of your collection that will produce the greatest return and least frustration. If you do get tired and quit, it is best if all of the high-value items have been either sold or allocated to be retained.

The first order of business is to select an area of the collection to work with. Then, you must understand what is necessary to either sell it effectively or determine which items should be kept. The obvious starting point would be to understand any guidance provided by the collector, either directly or indirectly. For example, a collector may have a documented group of high-value coins that clearly represents the concentration of value in his collection.

Keep in mind that if the collector did not provide such guidance directly, there may be indirect indications. For example, coins placed in a safety deposit box are likely to be more valuable than those in a box in a desk drawer.

If you are lacking specific guidance from the collector, the following general recommendations might work well for you with respect to focusing your attention on various portions of the collection. In general, the greatest concentration of value in a typical collection is likely to be with

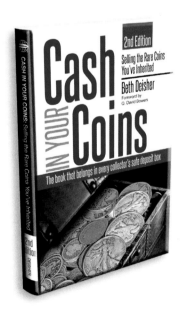

Cash in Your Coins: Selling the Rare Coins You've Inherited is a potentially useful book for those attempting to identify their newly inherited coin collection.

coins containing precious metals and coins of higher denominations. That is not to say that there are not very high-value lower-denomination coins; for example, there are cents worth hundreds of thousands of dollars. But it is more likely that you will find high-value silver dollars than high-value cents, nickels, or dimes. Likewise, it is more likely that solid gold coins will be more valuable than copper and nickel coins. These generalizations should enable you to identify portions of your collection of higher value, thus providing you with a good place to start. You can then work your way down the denominations as time permits and as your interest is sustained.

RECOMMENDED SEQUENCE OF ATTENTION IN LIEU OF DIRECT GUIDANCE

1. **Gold coins.** The precious-metal value alone will likely place such items among your most valuable. With the price of gold at about $1,100 per ounce, even a 1/10-ounce gold coin is worth $110 for precious-metal content. And a $20 gold piece (the federally issued examples of which are known as double eagles), which contain just under one ounce of gold, would be worth $1,100. As these examples demonstrate, any gold coins are certainly a good starting point.

2. **Silver dollars.** Next to gold coins, silver dollars are usually highest in value. This would include Peace, Morgan, Liberty Seated, Draped Bust, and Flowing Hair dollars, as well as trade dollars. All of these types are solid silver and contain almost one ounce of the precious metal. More importantly, most silver dollars have numismatic values higher than their bullion content. Many of the less-common dates and date/mintmark combinations are of higher value, especially in higher grades. Silver dollars can be worth hundreds, thousands, and even hundreds of thousands of dollars.

3. **Silver half dollars.** Quite often, there is considerable value in these silver coins. This includes coins of the Franklin, Liberty Walking, Barber, Liberty Seated, Draped Bust, and Flowing Hair designs.

4. **Lower denominations.** This category includes both dimes and quarters of the Barber, Liberty Seated, Draped Bust, and Flowing Hair designs; twenty-cent pieces; half dimes; Shield, Liberty Head, and Buffalo nickels; two- and three-cent pieces; large cents; Flying Eagle and Indian Head small cents; and half cents. These items often have considerable numismatic value.

5. **Common-date silver dimes and quarters.** This includes Mercury dimes, early (pre-1965) Roosevelt dimes, and Washington quarters. These items are easy to transact based on their bullion value, but since they are smaller denominations, it takes many more coins to amount to an ounce of silver.

6. **Common-date nickels and small cents.** Other than key-date issues, most items in this category—which includes Jefferson nickels and Lincoln cents—have too low a value to justify much effort due to the transaction costs that occur.

7. **Government-issued sets.** Many government-issued coin sets are worth only a few dollars and often are worth less than their original issue price. These items were manufactured in large quantities, sold at premium prices, and generally kept intact since they are purchased specifically by collectors.

8. **Foreign coins (excepting bullion).** Most foreign base-metal coins hold little value. Gold and silver coins would be an exception, and coins gathered by specialists who acquired them with substantial knowledge may be as well.

Gold coins and silver dollars are the most likely coins in a collection to have significant worth.

By working with the collection one portion at a time and starting with the highest-value portions first, you are able to judge the return on your investment of time, as well as your enjoyment of the process. When you reach a point where the return and enjoyment is outweighed by your effort, you can stop and take a simplified approach for the remainder, accepting a poor return but knowing that you have done well on the major portions where value is concentrated.

For example, you might be able to sell the first $90,000 of a $100,000 collection with an acceptable level of effort, obtaining reasonable and fair value, and then sell the remaining $10,000 worth for 50¢ on the dollar in a single bulk transaction. In that way, you have achieved an optimal return given the amount of time you are willing to spend. Approached in this manner, the poor return on the last $10,000 worth sold is insignificant compared to the solid return on the first $90,000.

CASE STUDY: MARY INHERITS HER FATHER'S COLLECTION

Mary remembers from her childhood the amount of time her father spent sitting at his desk examining his coin collection. She also remembers his continuous efforts to develop her interest.

Her interest never materialized, but the recent passing of her father has left her with the task of handling the disposition of his collection. Mary is the older of two children and the executor of her father's estate. Her brother, Peter, has no interest in coin collecting either and is struggling financially.

Both Mary and Peter recognize the significance of coin collecting to their father and want to honor it in some way, but they have struggled to define an approach.

Unfortunately, Mary's father—though well-intentioned—had never taken the time to completely catalog his collection, and he did not provide any guidance as to how to dispose of it. He did not even provide any guidance as to what coins might contain more significance to the family.

His collection consisted of thousands of pieces, some clearly valuable and others that did not appear to be worth very much stuffed in boxes. Mary decided to start by taking a representative sample to a local coin dealer. On her first visit, she received an offer to purchase the coins she had brought with her. She quickly realized that she had no basis on which to evaluate the fairness of the offer. She therefore decided to pass on the offer and subsequently seek some knowledge that would better equip her to sell her coins at fair value.

Mary conducted some Internet research on selling coins and attempted to gain some rough valuations based on recent transactions. She compared these results with the offer made by the local dealer and quickly realized that the more knowledge she could acquire, the better she would do at realizing a fair price.

Her collection contained a small number of gold coins and older silver dollars. Mary decided to catalog these as best she could and identify the market values via price guides. She then compared those values with recent auction results and derived what she considered fair values.

She took those coins to the local dealer and was able to negotiate a price she considered fair for a portion of the coins and received a check on the spot. For a few of the coins, however, she

Mary prioritized the gold coins and silver dollars in her late father's collection, as those were the most likely pieces to provide significant return.

was not satisfied with the price she could get from the dealer, and so she decided to try to auction them.

After completing her sales of the gold coins and silver dollars, Mary shifted her attention to the silver half dollars and quarters in the collection and took the same approach to their liquidation. Though Mary felt she was selling the coins at fair value, she did not really enjoy the process, and she noted that the proceeds on the lower-denomination coins were significantly less.

Having sold a significant portion of the collection, Mary looked at what remained and decided to explore the buy ads in a weekly numismatic newspaper. She recognized quickly that she could sell many of the common lower-value items, such as Mint sets and bulk small cents and nickels, at about 60 to 70% of what price guides listed. She decided that a quick transaction at those prices would meet her needs and that she did not wish to spend more time on it.

During the process of selling the coins, Mary had set aside a few coins which she had remembered seeing during her childhood. She decided that she would like to retain these coins to honor her father's memory.

As a result of her experience selling coins, she was able to assess a fair real-market value for the coins she wished to retain. She was then able to divide the resulting proceeds with her brother, fairly accounting for the coins she kept.

Mary had struck the right balance in terms of the use of her time and the results she obtained in liquidating the collection. Mary's time was valuable, and even if she could have received a higher return on some of the coins with more effort on the sale, she chose to apply some common sense so that she did not expend an effort inconsistent with the benefits.

Mary's preparation, research, and close work with a reputable coin dealer allowed her to liquidate a portion of the collection for a good return and also retain some pieces which would serve as mementos of her father.

It is vital to gain a basic understanding of coin collecting in order to effectively manage an inherited collection, as you must immediately deal with preservation and protection of the collection and then gradually focus on its disposition.

CHAPTER 10

For the Inheritor: Important Knowledge You Will Need

If you have no experience with coin collecting, it is strongly recommended that you obtain a good book covering all of the basics. An excellent choice is *The Coin Collector's Survival Manual*, authored by Scott Travers. This book covers grading, buying and selling, protection, and preservation. It is an excellent starting point to acquire knowledge, and an interesting read. Another award-winning volume is *The Expert's Guide to Collecting and Investing in Rare Coins*, by Q. David Bowers.

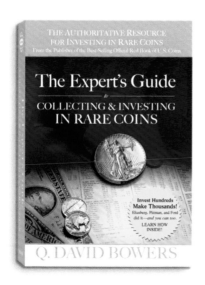

Q. David Bowers's *The Expert's Guide to Collecting and Investing in Rare Coins* isn't only good for experts; even the heir with no prior experience in numismatics will find this work invaluable.

* * * * *

Once you have built the foundation of your knowledge generally, you will need to gain more specific knowledge with respect to the collection you have inherited. The composition of the collection will determine what additional knowledge is required. For this you will need to examine the inventory, assuming one exists. It is first recommended that you categorize your collection based on concentration of value. This will naturally lead to certain recommended sales approaches later on.

An initial categorization might be:

- Gold coins, which are inherently valuable based on melt value alone
- Silver dollars, including those of the Morgan, Peace, trade, and Liberty Seated designs
- Silver half dollars, including those of the Liberty Walking, Franklin, and Barber designs
- Liberty Seated and Barber coins of lower denominations (half dimes, dimes, twenty-cent pieces, and quarters), as these are all made of silver
- Coin series in which the collector may have specialized, such as large cents
- Bulk base-metal (copper, nickel, etc.) coins, such as Lincoln, Wheat Ears Reverse cents; Indian Head cents; and Buffalo nickels
- Modern coins, individual or in rolls or bags
- U.S. Mint sets
- Foreign coins
- Exonumia (non-coin items) such as medals and tokens

The collection you inherited may contain coins in some or all of these categories. Some categories may be represented by only a few specimens, and others might have many. Generally, you will want to start at the top (gold coins and silver dollars) and work your way down, time permitting.

Once you have categorized the collection, it may be worthwhile to acquire some specific knowledge of your particular coins and/or the series to which they pertain. For example, do you have many higher-value coins that are not professionally graded? If that is the case, you may wish to purchase a grading guide so that you are somewhat familiar with the grading parameters for the coins you have. In that way, you can look at a table of values, bracket possible grade ranges, and determine if certification is a worthwhile expense.

If the collector was a specialist and had extensive holdings within a particular series—such as large cents or Barber coinage—you might find it worthwhile to obtain a book specific to that series.

If your inherited collection contains many coins of the same denomination or series, it may serve you well to gain additional knowledge on that subset of coins.

✦ ✦ ✦ ✦ ✦

SHOULD YOU HAVE THE COINS PROFESSIONALLY GRADED?

In general, knowing the precise grade when you sell a coin is very important, as purchasers will be very conservative on grade assumptions, and small grade changes can dramatically affect price.

If you have coins that are not graded, you can send them in to a professional third-party certification company such as NGC or PCGS, but certification can be expensive, and it is only warranted if the potential value justifies the expense. For example, if you have a common-date Morgan dollar that is worth $50 at MS-60, $60 at MS-63, and $75 at MS-64, and certification costs $15, it may well not be worthwhile unless you are quite sure it will be graded MS-64 or higher. On the other hand, if the MS-60 price is $200, the MS-63 price $400, and the MS-64 price $825, grade certainty would be very cost effective. You should acquire sufficient knowledge to be able to estimate grade so that a values table will be able to provide you with low/high estimates that you can then weigh against the costs of certification.

To be conservative, you might take a step-by-step approach, having 10 coins certified based on your analysis and then studying the results to see if it was a worthwhile expense. Based on a careful analysis of your first certification effort, you can then decide if proceeding appears worthwhile.

HANDLING SUBSET SPECIALTY COLLECTIONS

If it appears the collector concentrated on a specialized niche of numismatics, you will need to learn some specifics of this area in order to equip yourself to deal with the collection effectively.

Die varieties and error coins. Some specialists focus on acquiring die varieties and errors that occurred at the mint during manufacturing. A coin may have been incorrectly stamped such that the design is not in the proper place. The die may have been cracked, resulting in visible modifications to the design. In some cases, parts of the design may be missing completely. Other errors occur when some impurity on the die results in extraneous detail on the design. In still other instances, the material used as the blank is incorrect or defective.

There is essentially an infinite variety of possible die varieties and errors affecting different types. However, these coins can be a challenge to sell, as many coin collectors do not collect them and there is far less pricing information available for them. For regular coins, there are several widely available market-value guides that can provide a wealth of information to the collector. With regard to die varieties and error coins, there are only a few guides, and these are not as frequently updated.

Once you believe you have an approximate understanding of value, you can get in touch with dealers who focus on die varieties and error coins and buy and sell them regularly.

The 1955 doubled-die obverse Lincoln cent is among the most popular and well-known die varieties in the hobby.

Pattern coins. Pattern coins are made as examples of possible future coins. Their designs are preliminary and frequently are changed before any coins are minted for circulation (if at all). Typically, they were made in very small quantities; thus, even though the collecting community for patterns is small, their value can be very high. Since these items are typically of high value, they can be sold in a manner similar to high-value regular-issue coins.

This 1859 pattern half dollar (Judd-238) is one of hundreds of ultra-rare "test" coins for which specialty collectors clamor.

◆　◆　◆　◆　◆

Tokens, hobo nickels, medals. In addition to official coins, many coin collectors acquire items similar to coins. Medals are produced both by the U.S. Mint and by private companies to commemorate events. They are sometimes minted using precious metal. Tokens have been issued by a variety of organizations and private firms and individuals at various periods of time. Civil War tokens, Hard Times tokens, and transportation tokens are some of the more common varieties. Token collecting is a detail-oriented specialty, and if you have a number of items in your collection that you cannot identify, you may need to acquire some books to aid in your research.

One approach to identification is a precisely crafted Internet search including whatever wording you can read on the item. Quite often this will lead to a picture that you can use to identify it. Hobo nickels are Buffalo nickels that were modified by an artist (frequently to make the Indian into the likeness of a stereotypical hobo), and these too have their own very specialized collecting community (the Original Hobo Nickel Society).

Tokens, hobo nickels, and Mint medals are frequently
part of coin collections.

✦ ✦ ✦ ✦ ✦

Elongated coins. Elongated coins have been made using many standard circulating coins and their designs and also with proprietary designs. Elongated coins are typically coins that were minted as normal circular metal coins, but they are placed in a machine that applies sufficient pressure to stretch them in one or more dimensions, typically producing an oval as the final shape. These machines are often found at museums, theme parks, and other tourist spots.

This elongated coin—created by stretching and overstamping an Indian Head cent—is a souvenir from the original San Francisco Post Office.

◆　◆　◆　◆　◆

Colonial coins. You may find your collection contains coins dated earlier than 1793, issued privately or by colonial governments. Many of the original 13 colonies issued coinage from the 1600s to late 1700s. These items are often quite worn, but they may be very valuable nonetheless. Since they may be worth a considerable amount, it is very important that you don't attempt to clean or alter their surfaces in any way.

Some collections also include numismatic books, minting dies, and other specialized items. Some of these may be of high value, but they are likely to take more time to research, value, and sell due to their specialized nature.

Wood's Hibernia farthings such as this one were not popular in Ireland, the nation for which they were minted, and thus were shipped to the American colonies and used in commerce there.

◆　◆　◆　◆　◆

In general, once you identify sections of the collection that are composed of items in one of these numismatic subsets, you will want to conduct some research to learn the possible ways to proceed. A good starting point is the Internet; for most specialized collecting areas, there are Internet communities that can provide a wealth of information. A small amount of research will likely provide you with the names of some dealers who focus on the specialty, as well as some guidance on how to value them. Understanding the history surrounding the items will also assist you in deciding whether to sell these items or to retain them.

If you do decide to sell, you will most likely use sales approaches similar to those used for the remainder of your collection, with a specific method being chosen based on the value of the individual items.

SPECIAL SECTION: COIN GRADING

It is important to understand a few basics about the grading of coins. Coins are often described as Good, Very Good, Fine, Very Fine, etc. Unfortunately the words used to describe a coin can be misleading. For example, a Very Good coin is really not "very good" at all in the traditional sense of the term. Coins are graded on a scale from 1 to 70. A "Good" coin receives a grade of 4 or 6—at the bottom of the scale. Grades of 60 to 70 are reserved for coins that have never been circulated and exhibit no wear.

Of course, a coin graded 60 may be very unattractive and loaded with marks from banging around in bags, but it does not show any circulation wear. A coin graded 70 is perfect and has no defects. Grades below 60 are used to describe coins that have been circulated. The highest such grade currently in use is AU-58 (About Uncirculated) and is assigned to coins which have extremely little wear. A Good-4 coin has full rims and a readable date but only an outline of the major design, lacking all detail such as strands of hair, feathers, etc.

A Standing Liberty quarter graded VG-8 is not "very good" in that it shows very obvious wear and a near-complete lack of detail.

◆ ◆ ◆ ◆ ◆

With some education, you should be able to determine an approximate grade for circulated coins. However, for uncirculated coins, distinguishing grade is much more difficult and best left to the professionals especially if major value fluctuations exist.

Grades also often contain prefixes and suffixes. There are two primary manufacturing processes used at the Mint: that for circulation strikes and that for Proof strikes. Proof coins are manufactured for collectors and those of the modern era have a mirror-like finish. They are normally found in grades from PF-60 to PF-70, though sometimes Proof coins are mishandled and exhibit wear, in which case they are referred to as "impaired"

Proofs. Circulation-strike coins are those made for circulation. In the grade range from 60 to 70, they are preceded by MS (MS-60 to MS-70). MS stands for Mint State, indicating a coin exactly as it was produced.

In some instances, grades have suffixes that indicate additional information. For example, high-grade copper and bronze coins often have a suffix of RD, RB, or BN, standing for red, red-brown, and brown, respectively. Red coins exhibit the original copper color typical of new coins, whereas Brown coins have lost their copper color with age. Red-Brown coins have a combination of brown and copper coloring. Other suffixes are used to indicate high-value characteristics, such as FBL (full bell lines) on Franklin half dollars or DMPL (deep mirror prooflike surfaces) on circulation-strike coins that were minted early in the lifespan of a die.

Depending on your interest, you may choose to learn about coin grading by reading one of the guides or by taking a course, but in any case you need to at least familiarize yourself with the terminology.

For guidance on grading some of the most commonly encountered classic U.S. coins, see the appendix.

This Franklin half dollar was graded MS-65 FBL, as the bell lines on the reverse remain intact in their entirety.

Selling a collection at a fair value is very challenging.

CHAPTER 11

For the Inheritor: Disposing of Your Collection

You may decide that a sale of all or part of your collection is warranted. It is important to select the best method for selling your coins and also to invest most of your time in marketing those portions of your collection that are most valuable. Start by dividing a collection into two categories, one for higher-value coins and the other for lower-value coins.

Sample higher-value items would include:

- Individual coins worth more than $50
- Certified coins
- A group of coins with substantial bullion value
- Coin albums (completely or partially filled)

Certified coins—especially gold coins, such as this half eagle—are more likely to hold significant value.

Sample lower-value items would include:

- Individual coins worth less than $50
- Government-issued sets (Proof and Mint sets)
- Coin rolls
- Low-grade bulk cents, nickels, and dimes

Disclaimer: The discussion of sales methods throughout the remainder of this section is intended to make you aware of the possibilities rather than provide strict instructions on how to sell each type of coin. The best approach and available venues may change with time, and you need to select approaches consistent with your skills. When you actually go to sell some coins, you should explore all possible alternative sales techniques while staying within the amount of time you are willing to devote. You should also conduct a few smaller transactions to gain experience with selling effectively. This will enable you to find your personal most effective method and allow you to proceed with confidence.

As described previously, when you embark on the sale of your collection, you really don't know how enjoyable the process will be and how you will do financially. Thus you should initially focus on the higher-value items that are likely to produce more value and less frustration.

Each category of coin is best sold using a method that is likely to produce a good return. The remaining chapters in this section will describe a variety of sales methods for each category. The best method for you will be determined by a number of factors. The quantity of coins and overall value are two very important parameters; if your collection is of sufficient value, you may be able to participate in a major auction or justify the travel expense of a dealer visit.

On the other hand, if your collection is of more modest value or mostly populated by average-value items, you will need to utilize a variety of methods. Your geographical location is important as well. For example, you may live in or near a large city with several major coin dealers, or you may live in a rural area with no coin dealers or just a local jewelry shop that also sells coins.

One important point is not to be afraid to mail coins to reputable dealers using the United States Postal Service. Coins may be easily mailed at relatively low cost. Flat-rate Priority Mail is a very good choice, as it enables you to mail 70 pounds of coins for about $10 anywhere in the United States. Postal insurance is relatively inexpensive, so you will want to be sure that you adequately insure the items you are mailing.

As long as you are sending your coins to a reputable dealer or certification company, there is no need to worry about the coins being switched or taken by the receiver. It is reassuring if the dealers you interface with are members of the Professional Numismatists Guild (PNG). Similarly, only use the major professional third-party certification companies (NGC, PCGS, ANACS, and ICG).

A good way to sell coins to a mail-order dealer is to start with a small transaction and increase the size as your confidence in the dealer grows. If the dealer pays quickly and at the expected level as advertised in his buy ads, that is a good start.

One other point that is good to keep in mind is that sometimes the first dealer you speak with may be the bearer of bad news. You might have many common items in your collection (government-issued sets, modern coins) that are worth considerably less than indicated by the value guides due to the fact that they are widely available in great numbers. Their low values are diminished by transaction costs, too. A reputable dealer will inform you of this "bad news," but that is not a sign that you should go elsewhere. The best way to gain confidence with a dealer to whom you may decide to sell some coins is to confirm the recommendations and information he is providing with other numismatic sources. For example, the values of common-date government-issued sets may be easily found by looking at want ads in the back of a current issue of a numismatic publication.

Assuming you're working with a trustworthy dealer, shipping your coins via the USPS can be a reliable and cost-effective way of doing business.

Most of the value in your collection is likely to be concentrated in a relatively small number of coins.

CHAPTER 12

For the Inheritor: Selling High-Value Portions of the Collection

Those coins in your collection that are of high value are where most of the potential return is concentrated, and therefore these pieces are most deserving of your attention. It is these coins that offer the greatest opportunity for gain. However, when not treated and sold properly, they may be the source of your greatest loss in value.

There are a couple important general guidelines. First, coins that are individually worth more than $250 should always be certified prior to sale. If you sell uncertified coins for which values can change substantially with single-step changes in grade, it is highly likely that the dealer will pay a price based on the lower grade rather than the higher. This is not because the dealer is dishonest, but instead because a sensible businessman is not going to take any grade risk when purchasing a coin. Grading coins is an imperfect process, and even a very experienced coin dealer can be surprised by the grade assigned by a certification company. Therefore, the dealer is going to buy the coin at the price point of the lowest possible grade that it would likely certify at.

Therefore, when you sell high-value uncertified coins, it is possible you will receive substantially less than the real value of the coin. Depending on the actual grade that would be assigned by a certification service and how far away that is from the dealer's estimated lowest grade, you might receive anywhere from 10 to 90 cents on the dollar. If you are going to sell high-value coins, it is well worth it to spend the time and money to have them certified so that you receive fair value when they are sold.

More valuable coins can be sold in a number of ways, including:

- ◆ Outright sale to a dealer
- ◆ Consignment sale to a dealer
- ◆ Consignment to a major auction
- ◆ Consignment to daily coin auctions

The method selected may result in very different results, as in some cases the inheritor is taking the "inventory risk," while in others that is transferred to the dealer in return for immediate payment.

Any coin that you can safely assume would sell for more than $250 should be certified before sale. Imagine selling an uncertified 1882 half eagle to a dealer who conservatively estimates its grade to be MS-64; you would expect a wholesale price below the retail value–$1,400 according to the first edition of the *Guide Book of United States Coins, Deluxe Edition*. If you instead had it certified and it was graded MS-65, it would be valued at closer to $4,000–and you'd be leaving more than $2,000 on the table!

⬩ ⬩ ⬩ ⬩ ⬩

WORKING WITH A DEALER (OUTRIGHT SALE OR CONSIGNMENT)

When you buy and sell stocks in the stock market, the transaction occurs instantly at a price known to both buyer and seller, so there is no risk that results from the passage of time occurring between the purchase and sale of a share of stock. When transacting collectibles, however, inventory risk is a major consideration. When a dealer buys a coin, he does not know if he will sell it to a collector tomorrow or in three months. During this period, the coin could go up or down in value, and that is what produces inventory risk.

For example, if a dealer purchases an expensive coin outright at 90% of market value and the value drops 10% prior to sale, he makes no profit. As a result of this potential loss, a dealer will likely pay less when he takes on inventory risk in order to compensate him for taking this risk. Conversely, if a collector consigns his coins, the collector bears the risk of market-price fluctuations and also ties up his own funds (as opposed to the dealer's) during the period that elapses prior to sale. Therefore, you can expect a higher return on a consignment sale to compensate you for bearing this risk.

There is also inventory risk inherent in bullion transactions, as even though the time between purchase and sale may be only a day or so, sometimes bullion prices fluctuate wildly. In such periods of volatility, substantial losses could be incurred.

Of the above four methods, outright sale to a dealer is easiest, results in the quickest payment, and shields the inheritor from inventory risk. Unfortunately, these advantages come with the price that this method likely returns the poorest result. The dealer is going to want to purchase the coin at a significant enough discount to the current market price to offset his inventory risk, and he will also want to be compensated for the opportunity cost of the cash he ties up.

One approach to dealer sales is to attend a coin show with a large number of major dealers present. This affords you the opportunity of shopping your coins with many dealers, as you will not be limited to the few who may be located near your home. If you do attend a coin show, you should be aware that coin dealers are primarily there to conduct business, as attendance is costly. You should approach them with a clear understanding of your purpose and have reasonable expectations. It is not likely they will be willing to spend a significant amount of time educating you. You will be most successful if you present coins you would like to sell to dealers who deal in those specific items.

You will likely benefit from some advance research. This can take several forms. You might search numismatic publications to locate dealers seeking to buy coins. You should look at their ads and/or Web sites to determine which dealers focus on the kinds of coins you are trying to sell. If you believe you have found some dealers with whom you could potentially do business, contact them before the show to determine their interest in meeting at the show, confirm when they will be present, and determine times that are most convenient for them.

It takes time and effort to sell coins, and during this time, market values can rise and fall. In the case of outright sale to a dealer, this risk is borne by the dealer, whereas in consignment methods, this risk is borne by the inheritor. It is only fair, therefore, that such risk will diminish the price paid by a dealer.

Outright dealer sales may be the best choice if proceeds are needed quickly and available time is short. In those cases, it is very important that the inheritor have a solid understanding of the market value of the coins being sold so that he is aware of the profit margin and is comfortable with it. All valuable coins should be certified so that the grade does not create uncertainty, as it is unlikely a dealer will want to take on any grade risk, and ungraded coins are likely to be assessed at the lowest grade a dealer is sure the coin will be graded by a certification service.

Once the grade is established, the collector should be aware of both retail and wholesale prices. The annually issued *Handbook of United States Coins* ("Blue Book") is a wholesale ("buy price") version of the Red Book. The more frequently issued Greysheet publishes values representing what dealers are paying for coins that they buy and also the prices for which they sell these coins. For scarce coins, you would like to realize an amount very close to retail price. For common coins, you are likely to be much closer to wholesale pricing. Also, it is recommended that you take the coins to several dealers seeking a best offer. As a general guideline, you should not accept any offers that are less than 70% of retail value unless you have extensively researched the matter and are convinced this represents fair value.

If you do decide to pursue an outright dealer sale, you should not limit yourself to dealers in your community or otherwise nearby. Many collectors live in regions with direct access to only a few dealers, and limiting yourself to only these dealers may not produce the best results. You should not hesitate to mail coins to more distant dealers, assuming you are sure to select dealers that are members of the Professional Numismatists Guild and other reputable business organizations, preferably with references from other collectors or other recommendations. By broadening the set

Using the Internet to scope out dealers with whom you might work is a prudent step to take before approaching any particular outlet.

of dealers you would consider for the sale, you can obtain several estimates and work with just those who seem most interested in your collection. Some dealers specialize in certain coin series and are more likely to sell the coins they buy directly to other collectors, whereas some other dealers will wholesale them to other dealers. Whenever a dealer wholesales the items, you are adding another layer to the transaction that will result in an additional profit to some other individual, thus reducing your proceeds.

Many dealers, recognizing the reluctance of collectors to mail their coins, provide free mailing boxes with delivery confirmation. If your collection is large enough, some dealers may be willing to travel to your home to pursue the transaction.

If you are fortunate to live in or near a city with many coin dealers, you may have the luxury of accomplishing this shopping process in-person, rather than through the mail. This does make it simpler, and it also reduces the time it takes to make progress. Take a representative sample of your collection to several dealers and get their best offers. Don't sell the items right away. After you receive several offers, compare these with the price guides and understand the difference in prices. If you enjoyed your interaction with a particular dealer, discuss your findings and see if

Establishing a good working relationship with a friendly dealer can pay huge dividends in the course of your disposition.

an accommodation can be made. A good dealer should be willing to tell you if there are portions of your collection that he cannot buy effectively and suggest alternative approaches.

Once you establish a working relationship with a dealer, you can enlist his aid in your sales process, but you should verify that results are acceptable for you each step along the way. You should have a general discussion of which coins should be certified as well as the sales approaches he is open to, such as consignment sales. Select a dealer who makes sense for you, who is comfortable to deal with, and who has selling experience that is relevant to your collection. Examine the sales inventory of the dealer you choose, as you will undoubtedly find some of the same items you are selling. You will therefore have an opportunity to understand his profit margins and decide if they are acceptable to you.

CONSIGNING YOUR COINS TO AN AUCTION

Some collectors will have a number of high-value coins, and this may create the opportunity to work with a major auction house. There are a number of auction houses throughout the United States which regularly auction millions of dollars worth of coins in one venue. Sometimes they auction the entire collection of one collector, producing a color catalog dedicated to this particular collection. More commonly, the auction house assembles many high-value coins from a large number of collectors and auctions them together, spreading the overhead of the auction over a large base.

Auctions are a major buying venue for serious collectors and dealers, and the auction house has a strong incentive to maximize the return for their clients. The track record of an auction house producing good return on the items they auction will assure a continual flow of future clients. Quite often, an auction will produce prices substantially higher than the price guides and command a lot of market attention in the numismatic trade press. If you have a number of high-value coins, you should contact one or two of the major auction houses to determine if they are an appropriate venue for your sale.

Of course, many collectors' collections will not contain sufficient high-value items to gain attention from an auction house. In these instances there are other choices.

One choice worth exploring is an online auction operated by an auction company that specializes in numismatic items. Tens of thousands of coins are sold via these auctions each year. The various companies' Web sites typically provide users with the ability to search recent auctions. This

Larger collections with lots of high-value items might be best sold through auction houses.

✦ ✦ ✦ ✦ ✦

enables you to view auction results for the coins you are selling and determine likely sales proceeds. If you are satisfied with the net proceeds and the time it takes to receive payment, this can be an easy means of selling these coins.

Of course, no mention of auctions would be complete without a discussion of eBay. Though many, many coins are auctioned on eBay and some people do very well, use of this venue requires substantial experience and knowledge on your part. Most people don't really know what to expect as an eBay seller, and there is great potential for miscommunication between the buyer and seller. If you have an item graded by a certification company allowed by eBay (the venue allows coins graded by the major third-party grading firms, but not many smaller ones) or other items which can be sold without a certified grade based on accurate images, you may choose to experiment with his venue. This would be especially true if you enjoy the excitement of participating in an auction.

If you do market coins on eBay, make sure to take high-quality scans or photographs that fairly represent the actual coin. Do not take scans at angles intended to mask defects; in fact, it is better to do your best to highlight such defects visually and in your text to avoid surprises and disappointed buyers. Also, make sure to provide positive feedback to your buyers, as this will make it more likely they provide you with positive feedback. Pay close attention to the feedback you receive to assure that you are meeting buyers' expectations.

Selling low-value portions of a collection can require much time with a very small return.

CHAPTER 13

For the Inheritor: Selling Low-Value Portions of the Collection

Quite often, the portions of your collection that account for much of the volume and quantity of items actually amount to a much smaller part of the overall value. The fact that these items take up a lot of storage space and also represent a large quantity of individual coins often leads a person to spend far more time on them than they are worth.

For example, if you have 1,000 coins that are worth on average $1.50 each, you have a total achievable value of $1,500. Conversely, if you have 100 coins with an average value of $200 each, you have a potential realizable value of $20,000. The 100 high-value coins might be stored in one or two albums or a single safety deposit box, whereas the 1,000 low-value coins might fill several large boxes. The face value of the low-value coins might be a significant fraction of the realizable value, perhaps as much as 1/3. Unfortunately, to achieve fair value for these 1,000 coins might necessitate you spending considerable time, and it may well not be worth your time. Focus on the high-value portions of your collection first; if you are able to optimize those transactions, there is a far greater return on the investment of your time.

When selling the lower-value portions of your collection, the large number of items coupled with a low per-item value creates a difficult challenge of balancing the value to be received and the effort you expend. For some people, there may be sufficient interest in the process that the enjoyment justifies the expenditure of much more time than the value warrants.

For most inheritors, however, part of the objective is to attain fair value as quickly as possible. Most inheritors are not really interested in working with the collection and do not gain enjoyment from the process. In many instances, they are still employed and could spend their time on more productive, relaxing, or lucrative activities. At the same time, they recognize the effort expended by the collector over many years and would like

Large amounts of lower-value coins can take up a lot of room and would
require considerable effort and time to dispose of one-by-one.

♦ ♦ ♦ ♦ ♦

to honor that effort by receiving fair value for the sale. Approaching the
sales process in a smart fashion is most likely to provide the best balance.

For the low-value portions of the collection, this requires taking a good
look at the potential value and your own willingness to liquidate some
portions at relatively low valuations that may be appropriate given the
investment of time that would be required to achieve higher returns.

If you have a large bulk of low-value coins, a good place to start is the "Wanted" section at the back of most weekly coin newspapers. There you will see a number of dealers advertising buy prices for low-value items. This is one of the easiest ways to sell such material. All that needs to be done is to create an inventory, bundle it up, and mail it to the dealer. If the material is as requested, you should receive a check in a few weeks' time. After examining these ads, if you are able to receive a reasonable return on these low-value portions, you can simplify your effort by quickly selling these items.

Some of the portions of your collection may be too small to justify the transaction costs. You should first see if you can package these together to form a large enough bundle to send off to a mail-order buyer. Otherwise, you have several options:

Turn the coins in at face value to your local bank. This is often the best that can be achieved for small quantities of low-value coins for which any accounting of the real transaction costs would rule out a more significant effort.

Gifting coins to family members, especially younger ones, may draw them into the constructive hobby of coin collecting and thus help ensure the future of numismatics.

Give the coins away to family members or others to spur their interest in coin collecting. Though no financial return is received from gifting the coins, you may gain some personal satisfaction knowing that your family member who participated in the hobby would appreciate such a disposition. In the case of gifting the coins to family members, you are encouraging others to undertake the hobby that provided your ancestor with much enjoyment.

Place coins in circulation. Another great way to dispose of low-value coins is to place them in circulation by spending them in the normal course of your retail purchases. One of the reasons why coin collecting does not have many young participants is that it is difficult to find many older collectible coins in pocket change. During the first half of the 20th century, many of the more valuable and sought-after coins were found and pulled from circulation, and as a result, collector interest in searching pocket change was encouraged. Recently, circulation finds are more difficult, though not impossible, and as a result most desirable coins must be purchased or received in trade.

The State quarter program, which was initiated in 1999, illustrates the benefit of having collectible issues in circulation to the coin-collecting hobby in general. Since quarters are in circulation and there were 50 different state designs, all of a sudden young children could start assembling collections consisting of one quarter of each design. As a result of this interest, coin collecting thrived from 1999 to 2008, and the benefit was felt by almost all participants in the hobby. Dealers who sell supplies started selling many albums, holders, and educational materials. Coin values in general increased as participation grew, and some of the collectors who began by collecting State quarters went on to collect other coins.

The State quarters program, by introducing many new collectible designs into circulation, popularized the hobby amongst youngsters and benefited the coin collecting industry in general.

The Presidential dollars program, which began in 2007, also exhibits the importance of circulation finds, but in a different way. These issues, though struck in a variety of different designs, are not used widely in circulation and therefore cannot be collected in pocket change. As a result, this program has not provided the same benefit to coin collecting as the State quarter program.

While similar to the State quarters program in that it involves a number of different collectible designs released over a period of several years, the Presidential dollars program has not had the same positive impact on coin collecting due to the issues not being common in commerce.

✦ ✦ ✦ ✦ ✦

If you have a number of low-value collectible coins (Buffalo nickels; Lincoln, Wheat Ears Reverse cents; Indian Head cents; etc.) that are not of sufficient value to justify your time selling, the option of spending them introduces a supply of collectible items into circulation. A person receiving one of these items may be curious about their find and, as a result, be introduced to the hobby of coin collecting.

The best way to approach the release of a coin collection back into circulation is to spend them in a wide array of stores and at different times so that they are dispersed as widely as possible. It would be much better for 100 people each to find a coin or two rather than for a few people to find many coins. Effectively spending coins will produce the same return for you as turning them in to a bank, but with a larger benefit to the hobby.

You should view this as an opportunity to give back to the hobby that provided your ancestor with such great enjoyment over a long period of time. The end result will probably be a much greater sense of satisfaction than selling them to a dealer at a very low price point, yielding a small return.

SECTION III

For Collectors & Inheritors

Section III addresses a few general topics of interest to both collectors and inheritors. It is intended to provide you with basic awareness rather than detailed understanding of these areas.

As either a collector or inheritor, factoring in the impact of taxes is vital in properly managing a collection.

Chapter 14

Estate and Tax Considerations

Coin collections are often worth a significant amount of money, and sales therefore may result in significant tax consequences. Careful planning in advance can minimize taxes and increase the financial benefits you receive. It is not the intent of this work to present expert advice on estate or tax matters. These are complicated topics that should be addressed by a professional advisor familiar with your particular financial and family circumstances. Rather, the intent of this work is to make you aware of some of the considerations that a collector must be aware of when deciding how collections will be transferred.

Based on your analysis of the estate tax considerations, as well as the human considerations pertaining to your collection, you will ultimately have to decide whether you will transfer portions of your collection to your heirs and how you will do so.

ESTATE IMPACTS OF A COIN COLLECTION

A coin collection presents the executor of an estate with a number of challenges. Often, the executor—whether a family member or an otherwise trusted advisor—will lack knowledge of valuing a coin collection.

There are several reasons the executor will need to establish the market value of coin collections passing through probate:

- For purposes of estate tax calculations
- For purposes of fairly apportioning the collection to the heir
- For purposes of conveying to the heir the valuation basis of items they might sell in the future
- For purposes of liquidating the coin collection so that equal cash distributions will be provided to the heirs, should this be necessary

All of these needs basically require that the executor understand how the collection is organized and valued. While alive, the collector has the opportunity to greatly simplify the challenge faced by the executor by documenting the state of the collection, its valuation, and specific instructions for sales methodology and apportionment of items to be replaced.

Whatever means you use to catalog your collection, it is best to consider the specific information that would benefit your heirs:

- **Your understanding of valuation.** You know more than either your executor or heirs when it comes to coin values, so you can provide specific and detailed information as to where the value is concentrated in your collection and how best to establish market value. Be as specific as possible when documenting your valuations, referencing price guides along with your interpretations of the values they provide.
- **Your thoughts on apportionment.** If you would like to see a portion of your collection preserved, you should specifically identify the coins to be allocated to and preserved by each heir.
- **Your thoughts on sales methods.** If part of the collection is to be liquidated or sold, you are probably the best individual to recommend specific sales methodologies. Identify the best sales approach, as well as specific third parties you would choose to participate in the sale.

Since you will be paying taxes on the value you receive, market values should realistically assess the value of the coin and not represent inflated retail purchase prices.

Recording your thoughts and recommendations on the management of your collection is a critical step to undertake.

As in any other case, tax consequences should not govern your behavior. If selling your collection is best for your overall situation, then you should proceed with the sale. Awareness of the tax consequences should be used to assist you in obtaining an optimal result. You have invested your time and money over many years to assemble your collection, and the desired outcome is to transfer as much value as possible to your family members while at the same time minimizing the burdens they will feel in undertaking the liquidation or division of the collection.

AVOIDING THE ISSUE BY GIFTING

As in the case of any other asset, coin collections may be gifted during the lifetime of the collector, thereby avoiding transfer as a part of the estate and the resulting taxation. This requires advance planning and often results in a gradual gifting of portions of the collection within the guidelines of annual gift limitations imposed by the Internal Revenue Service (consult a tax advisor for the details of how such limitations might impact you). Approached in this manner, some or all of the collection value can bypass probate. Gifting should be seriously explored by all collectors planning to pass portions of their collection to an heir. In addition to the possible benefit of bypassing probate, there are several other advantages to gifting while you are alive.

When you gift coins while you are living, you are able to assist the heir in understanding the items they have received. They will become familiar with preserving and handling coins and also begin to understand the basics of coin collecting.

A second advantage is that you are greatly simplifying the work of your executor. All coins gifted prior to probate will not be dealt with by the executor, and thus his task is greatly simplified. Also, fair allocation is made easier, as the apportionment occurs while the collector is alive and can explain his rationale to everyone and secure the desired level of comfort and consensus.

A non-monetary benefit of gifting coins is that it may add to your enjoyment of the hobby after retirement by affording the opportunity to share your interest with one of your family members and build a long-lasting bond. It also may provide you with additional "manpower" to continue your collecting efforts and manage the collection's partial liquidation.

The only caution with regard to gifting items prior to your passing is that you will be trusting your heir to act according to your wishes for the management of these items (including the preservation, protection, and sale or retention) while you are still living.

A coin collection may have been a significant source of pride and enjoyment throughout the collector's life, and thus the collection can serve after his passing as a way for the family to remember the deceased.

CHAPTER 15

Other Considerations

Individual coins acquired throughout the years often have a long history and a special meaning to the collector and/or their family members. Coins may have been acquired continuously while traveling throughout the world. For example, military personnel will often acquire coins in the countries in which they are based and retain these as a part of a larger collection representing their service. It is also common for collections to be assembled around themes of interest to the collector. For example, coins may be a part of a Civil War memorabilia collection or included with an assortment of items tied to some other historical event. In still other instances, coins are passed down from generation to generation and thus may be one of the final remaining mementos of your ancestors.

In order to honor these memories, as well as potentially strengthen the connection between the collector and the heir, there are considerations beyond monetary value which should influence both parties' decisions on disposition of the collection. Obviously, both the collector and the heir will want to allocate these items in such a manner as to both provide optimal benefits to the family and also increase the likelihood that the items remain in your family indefinitely.

Of course, in some circumstances, financial realities will dictate that some portions of the collection cannot be maintained, but most families would benefit from retaining some key items with particular significance to the collector or his family.

As a collector, you should identify those coins with special significance and provide detailed information as to the reason for their importance when preparing your collection for inheritance. Apportionment of these items should be given particular attention. For example, if one heir would retain them whereas another would sell them, it would make sense to leave the coins to the heir who would retain them and allocate equivalent value in other assets to the remaining heirs.

Coins that are part of a memorabilia collection, that are associated with a specific time period, or that were otherwise of special importance to the collector deserve special consideration when it comes to disposition.

• • • • •

If you fail to identify and plan for the disposition of these items of significance while actively collecting, it is likely that these items will be lost in the effort of liquidating the larger collection and thus will receive no special consideration or treatment. When these items are disposed of without adequate planning, the opportunity to pass along significant heritage to children and grandchildren is lost. Here again, planning for these items while you are alive should be viewed as an enjoyable opportunity to connect with your loved ones in a manner different than your normal day-to-day interactions. Numismatics may provide your heirs with insight into your life beyond what they already know and thus serve as a vehicle for enhancement of your interactions as well as increased enjoyment of the hobby.

An inherited collection can be a priceless way to remember a loved one.

Several currents in the dynamic coin market warrant the attention of anyone dealing with a collection.

CHAPTER 16

Coin Industry Trends

There are a number of current trends in the "industry" side of the hobby that should be understood by anyone liquidating or consolidating a coin collection. This chapter provides an overview of these trends.

COIN GRADING AND CERTIFICATION

The assignment of grades to coins has been a major source of uncertainty with respect to coin collecting for many years. Since the value of a coin is substantially impacted by the grade it is assigned, accurate and consistent grading is essential to ensure you are buying and selling coins at fair prices.

In the 1980s, a number of companies began certifying and grading coins and placing them in sealed plastic holders. This was intended in part to eliminate grade uncertainty as a complicating aspect of coin transactions. Though this has worked to some degree, the subjective nature of coin grading has prevented certification from completely eliminating grade uncertainty as a factor in buying and selling coins. Numismatic publications have conducted studies on grading accuracy by submitting the same coins to several different certification companies. The results showed significant inconsistencies with grade assignments, the variance of which can substantially impact values.

"Premium" and "Plus" designations. No matter how many different certifications a coin may receive, many dealers and collectors feel a need to further refine the grade assignment by attaching designations intended to indicate that a coin is a strong representative of its grade and thus should command a premium value.

Through the years, there have been a variety of methods used to distinguish certified coins assigned otherwise identical grades.

Many coin dealers informally designate coins they are trying to sell as Premium Quality (PQ) examples of the coin's assigned grade and thereby justify in their own mind a higher market price. It is true that if one views a group of identically graded coins side-by-side, many collectors would agree which are more desirable coins. However, as these informal assignments are inconsistently applied by different dealers, other third-party approaches have recently emerged. For example, some services assign a "Plus" designation for coins they consider strong for the assigned grade.

This 1951 dime was graded MS-67+, as it was deemed to have exceptional quality for the grade.

· · · · ·

Shifting standards. Another problem is that over the years, generally accepted grading standards for some coin types can change. As a result, a coin correctly graded before a shift in standards might later be assigned a higher or lower grade (usually higher), which can affect its valuation.

Certification verification. A relatively new company started in 2007, the Certified Acceptance Corporation now takes certified coins, independently assesses them, and places a label on the slab if the coin is deemed to be high-end for its assigned grade.

Early and special-release coins. Recently, certification companies have started to define certain coins as "Early Release." For example, with the release of the National Baseball Hall of Fame commemoratives in 2014, coins received for grading by a certification firm by a certain date were designated as Early Release. Similarly, for the gold Kennedy half dollar, some coins sold at the 2014 American Numismatic Association World's Fair of Money were designated as Early Release items.

First Strike designations. Some certification companies designate a portion of a given year's newly minted coins as "First Strike," implying the design is more precisely represented since they are minted during the early part of the life of a coin die. However, many collectors would not be able to distinguish First Strike coins from those struck later, and the premiums currently applied to these coins may not be sustainable.

Perfect grades (MS-70 and PF-70). Most modern coins are minted with high quality standards and if individually packaged would attain a grade between MS-/PF-67 and MS-/PF-69, with a smaller percentage attaining a perfect grade of MS-/PF-70. Unfortunately, there is a high market premium being applied to these "perfect" coins assigned a grade of MS-70 or PF-70. In many instances, a collector might not be able to tell the difference between an MS-70 coin and one graded MS-68 or MS-69. But while the MS-68 and MS-69 coins typically are valued at a level similar to that of a typical ungraded coin purchased directly from the U.S. Mint, MS-70 coins are often valued at five to ten times the value of an MS-65 to MS-69 coin.

It is also true that most modern coins are not certified, so if these premiums for perfect coins do persist, that is likely to encourage more certification. That, in turn, may result in an increase in the supply of perfect-graded coins, which may result in lower values.

The CAC sticker on this Lincoln cent's slab indicates that the Certified Acceptance Corporation judges the coin to be high-end for NGC's assigned grade of MS-66RD.

"Early Release" designations, such as that received by this 2008 $10 American Buffalo gold bullion coin, are a new development in the coin collecting hobby.

This Proof American Silver Eagle was designated as a First Strike.

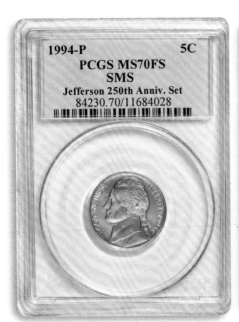

Coins receiving "perfect" grades of MS-70 or PF-70, as this Jefferson nickel did, carry a significant premium with some collectors.

REGISTRY SETS

Some collectors like to compete with other coin collectors to achieve a collecting objective—usually, a set of coins defined by series, date range, and/or variety. To facilitate this competition, NGC, PCGS, and several other companies provide Web sites where collectors may register their coins and, in doing so, compete with other collectors for the designation of the "best" set. In some instances, coins that are included in a registry set are designated as such when they are bought or sold. This is a relatively new phenomenon, and it is unclear whether the designations are indeed worth recording and will stand the test of time. It is particularly questionable as to whether such a designation should affect the coin's value.

Registry sets may be defined in an unlimited number of ways. A complete set of all date/mintmark combinations of a particular coin type and a "short set" consisting of one coin from each year for a coin type without regard to mintmark are two common definitions for a registry set. The definition of a registry set is primarily driven by collector interest. If there are collectors interested in particular sets, it is likely they will appear on

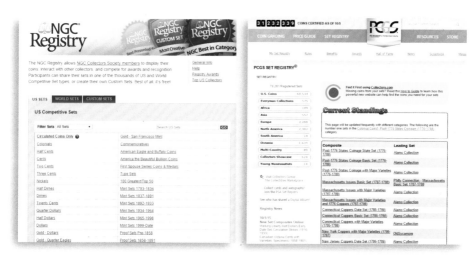

Both NGC and PCGS offer excellent online resources for those who are interested in registry sets and the friendly competition they foster.

a registry. Some registries require that coins be graded by a particular certification company.

Companies that maintain registries incorporate ranking systems devised by professional numismatists so that each set can be assigned a rank based on the coins it contains. The participants then compete for the highest rank.

BULLION VALUE FLUCTUATION

During periods of volatility in bullion prices—including that of the past few years—there can be substantial impact on coin collecting and numismatic values of coins. When bullion prices are very high, it may make sense to melt certain coins, diminishing their supply and hence resulting in an increase in their numismatic value. In other cases, higher bullion values will reduce the number of collectors who can afford to collect a particular series, resulting in diminished demand and lower numismatic premiums. After many decades of stagnation, bullion prices for precious metals shot up at the beginning of the 21st century, but they have since diminished substantially.

If you are interested in collecting coins for their bullion value, you should take the time to understand the historical variations in precious-metal spot prices and not be influenced by the never-ending advertisements of companies selling bullion to the public.

PROTECTION OF COINS FROM ENVIRONMENTAL DAMAGE

Historically, collectors have housed their coins in a variety of simple plastic or cardboard containers, as well as cabinet drawers. Each of these methods has some drawbacks and can result in wear and/or chemical deterioration of a coin's surface. Intercept Shield™ holders represent a technology intended to protect a coin from both wear and the environment on a long-term basis.

Hi! Sign in or register | Daily Deals

ebay

Shop by category ▾

My Feed

Collections

emarkable listing

Selling coins on eBay can be very enjoyable and also very profitable, and with substantial time available, you may be in a perfect position to take maximum advantage of this opportunity.

CHAPTER 17

Selling on eBay for Enjoyment and Profit

eBay auctions reach a very wide audience, ranging from experienced coin collectors and dealers to bidders with no knowledge or interest in coin collecting beyond a particular item. As a result, there are some items that can be sold on eBay at higher prices than would normally be achievable using other sales methods.

One advantage of selling on eBay is that you are able to search current and prior auctions for the item you are selling and learn what the item is selling for. You can also view the bid history and dynamics. You are likely to find a wide range of pricing outcomes for almost any individual item. This study of the sales history enables you to glean some sense of the likely results you can achieve by selling some of your coins on eBay.

The first step in deciding which coins to sell is to research recent sales. Compare the sale price realized to what could be obtained in a direct-to-dealer sale. Make sure to account for the eBay fee (10%) and PayPal fee (2 to 3%), as well as any shipping costs, when you calculate your net proceeds. Also examine the number of bidders and the bid history, as these serve as an indication of continued interest. For example, if an auction attracted six bidders with several competing near the final sales price, it is likely that there is continued demand for new auctions of the same item. If only two people were bidding, it may be worth trying to auction your coin, but this may indicate lesser demand. Also note the strategy of prior sellers. What was the starting price? Was there a reserve? Was there free or very low-cost shipping?

If as a result of your research you believe a coin may be worth auctioning on eBay, then it is worth a try. You will want to become familiar with the rules and successful techniques of eBay auctions. The last portion of this chapter will address how to auction coins on eBay and what to expect.

By using eBay's search refinement tools to sort out just the "sold listings," you can get a feel for the potential returns on an auction of your own.

◆ ◆ ◆ ◆ ◆ ◆

CAPITALIZING ON YOUR TIME FOR A QUICK PROFIT

As a retired collector with a lot of available time, you are perfectly positioned to profit from one particular kind of numismatic transaction. Each year, the U.S. Mint issues well more than a hundred new coins, counting all mintmarks, designs, finishes, and denominations. Most are available in quantities well in excess of demand and are thus destined to diminish in value from any initial surge back to the issue price and remain below cost for many years to come. However, each year there are a few issues that will only be available in quantities that are below expected demand, and it is these issues that offer very great short-term profit potential.

A few recent examples are the 2014 National Baseball Hall of Fame commemorative issues, as well as a variety of recent American Silver Eagle special issues (such as the Reverse Proof coins). Long before these issues may be actually purchased, they can be anticipated as likely to be in high demand. Though you cannot be sure exactly which of the Mint's many annual issues will be the ones to rocket up in value, there are a few indicators that can allow you to predict them.

First, exclude the regular annual issues. For example, each year the U.S. Mint issues standard sets, including Mint sets of all coins from the Philadelphia and Denver mints, a variety of Proof sets (including the standard Proof set and the silver Proof set), the America the Beautiful quarters set, the silver America the Beautiful quarters set, the Presidential dollars set, and other such issues. Since these sets are issued each year, the collector demand is well understood and a given year's set is not likely to greatly outperform similar issues of other recent years. Similarly, individual coins, such as a given year's standard Gold and Silver Eagles, are also unlikely to outperform similar issues from last year.

Eliminating these annual issues greatly reduces the possibilities for coins offering substantial investment return. Usually only a handful remain for analysis, including a few commemorative issues, a few special bullion coin issues or sets, and perhaps a few special individual issues of circulating coins.

When it comes to commemorative coins, most issues go down in value relative to the purchase price from the Mint. In order to offer short-term profit potential, two factors must be present. First, mintage must be limited to a quantity that is not likely to be enough to meet demand. Second, there must be something special about the topic/event commemorated or the manufacture of the coin that is likely to result in a very high demand. In 2014, two commemorative programs (a total of eight different coins, counting Proofs) were launched, the Civil Rights Act of 1964 and National Baseball Hall of Fame commemoratives. The Civil Rights Act commemorative followed the typical course of a coin, with supply equal to demand; however, the National Baseball Hall of Fame commemorative was released with a tremendous shortfall of supply relative to demand, resulting in the ability to sell the coin for premiums of 200 to 500% shortly after purchase. This situation was entirely predictable and was exploited by many collectors and dealers.

The National Baseball Hall of Fame commemoratives included a copper-nickel half dollar, silver dollar, and $5 gold piece and were made available in Proof and Uncirculated finishes. The highest mintage was for the low-cost copper-nickel half dollar issue, with lower mintages for the $5 gold piece and silver dollar. There are two factors that made it clear demand would be high for these coins. First, baseball is a very popular sport in the United States, so it could be expected that a commemorative celebrating the sport's hall of fame would find several markets outside of

The National Baseball Hall of Fame commemorative coins issued in 2014 (copper-nickel half dollar version shown) were popular with coin collectors and baseball fans alike, making for a hit on the market.

＊ ＊ ＊ ＊ ＊ ＊

the numismatic collector community. For example, collectors of sports memorabilia would find it a compelling item, and it also represented a very nice gift for young baseball enthusiasts. Second, these coins were manufactured as three-dimensional pieces, with concave and convex surfaces representing a ball and glove. This combination of a high-interest topic, special manufacturing technique, and relatively low mintage made it very likely that this issue would rise in value quickly.

Once you have identified what you think are the few issues likely to realize quick price appreciation, the availability of your time provides another advantage. The U.S. Mint also usually realizes when an issue is going to encounter high demand and establishes a special ordering process for these coins. Usually, sales begin at a specified time, and the Mint realizes that its Web site will not be able to handle the demand. To account for this, it invokes special procedures. For example, in the case of the National Baseball Hall of Fame commemorative, the U.S. Mint online store was shut down for 30 minutes before the commencement of sales. During that period, you could enter a queue to be allowed into the store once it reopened. The sooner you entered the queue, the shorter the wait would be. At the start of the process, entrants to the queue might receive wait times of 20 minutes or less, while later entrants encountered wait times of several hours.

Entering the queue at the earliest available opportunity provides you with the highest likelihood of being able to purchase the coin. Additionally, by monitoring the wait time of new queue entrants, you can confirm your projection of high interest prior to making the purchase.

The earlier you purchase, the quicker you are likely to receive the items and the sooner you can put them up for sale. For such high-interest items, early auctions are fueled by customers who were unable to purchase directly from the Mint and are seeking to obtain them as quickly as possible. Eventually, the prices do tend to settle down and usually diminish a bit, so the time to strike is as soon as possible.

It is likely that prior to receiving your coins, others will have already done so. In this interim period, you can search current and recent auctions to determine your asking price and likely return. Set the asking price somewhere near the highest recent auction results and set no reserve. Offering an auction with no reserve means that the item is likely to sell, hence those bidders who really want the item are strongly encouraged to participate, further stimulating bidding action. Keep shipping costs low and flat, as unknown or high shipping costs deter bidders.

MAXIMIZING YOUR PROFIT ON EBAY

A few general tips for getting the best returns possible:

Know when to certify your coins versus selling as-is. You will likely find both certified and uncertified coins on eBay. Many dealers who can expedite the certification process of their coins will realize great returns on coins certified MS-70 or PF-70, which command very high premiums. However, if you do not have a special arrangement for quick certification and also do not have any coins likely to receive perfect grades, you would be better off selling your coins directly as received rather than taking on the additional expense of certification and the risk of delay of the sale. Generally, a coin sold as purchased directly from the Mint will produce a comparable net return to those certified MS-69, PF-69, or below.

If your coin is likely to be graded MS-70 or PF-70 and you are able to have it certified quickly and affordably, you may be able to capitalize on the premiums associated with "perfect" grades. However, in most instances coins purchased from the Mint can easily be sold uncertified.

✦ ✦ ✦ ✦ ✦

Focus on gold and silver issues. Another lesson to be learned from the National Baseball Hall of Fame commemoratives is that the best return is likely to be made on gold and silver issues. Silver issues are the most widely collected of modern commemoratives and minted in moderate quantities relative to demand. Gold is less widely collected, as many cannot afford it, but typically is minted in very small numbers. Copper-nickel issues are made in very high quantities and while they may have high general-audience sales, they are the least sought-after in the numismatic secondary market, as any coin collector who wanted one generally could acquire it directly from the Mint.

Many modern commemorative programs consist of copper-nickel half dollar, silver dollar, and $5 gold piece issues. Focus on the silver dollars and $5 gold pieces if your goal is making a profit.

Pay attention to special-finish American Eagle issues. Another group of modern issues with predictable quick price appreciation has been American Eagles with special finishes, which have had some of the smaller mintages of this very popular series. The first example was the 1995-W American Silver Eagle, which was the only Eagle ever minted at the West Point Mint up to that time and was also only available as a part of the 10th-anniversary set that included the year's four Gold Eagles. Because of the expense of the set, the mintage was very low, and this coin is now worth thousands of dollars. More recent special-finish Eagles, such as the Reverse Proof issues, have also risen in price rapidly.

While American Silver Eagles are the coins that are most frequently released in Reverse Proof format, American Gold Eagles have been in the past as well, and the $50 American Buffalo gold coin was made in Reverse Proof in 2013.

* * * * *

Note the example of the 2014 gold Kennedy half dollar. The gold Kennedy half dollar—issued in commemoration of the 50th anniversary of the 1964 release of the Kennedy design—became one of these highly sought-after issues with quick price appreciation. John F. Kennedy is one of the most popular modern U.S. presidents, and his appeal is global. William R. Rice's *The Kennedy World in Medallic Art* was released around the same time as the coin, and the 2015 edition of the Red Book (issued in 2014) featured a Kennedy half dollar on its cover. Worldwide interest, coupled with the relative affordability of the gold issue, created an imbalance of supply and demand.

The gold Kennedy half dollars released in commemoration of the 50th anniversary of the design was a hugely popular issue.

✦ ✦ ✦ ✦ ✦

SELLING ON EBAY: OTHER IMPORTANT INFORMATION

If you have experience with selling items on eBay, offering your coins should be straightforward. There are only a few additional considerations, the most important being eBay's rules for representing your coins for sales. Read and familiarize yourself with eBay's rules for selling numismatic items. These are periodically updated, but the basics are as follows:

- Include good images of the actual item you are selling. These should faithfully represent the item and not hide defects. For example, if a coin has some unattractive toning, take magnified photographs of portions of that defect so that it is clear to the buyer.
- Represent the item accurately. For example, if an item is exactly as received from the U.S. Mint with all packaging and paperwork, say so, but if any of this is missing or damaged, indicate that as well. For recent Mint issues, the buyer will likely want to know if the certificate of authenticity (COA) is included. Similarly, if the packaging is torn or damaged, indicate as such and include a clear picture.
- Do not represent the grade of the coin unless it is certified and that certification is in accordance with eBay rules. eBay has strict rules on which certification companies are acceptable. If you have a coin certified by a company acceptable to eBay, you typically can represent it as such, but otherwise it is best to include something like "see pictures" in the item description and provide as high-quality a set of

images as possible. If the coin is of high value, you may find it worthwhile to have it certified by a company acceptable to eBay so that it can be more precisely represented.

♦ Make sure your shipping cost and options include insurance for numismatic items, as some of the insurance options exclude coins.

If you do sell coins on eBay, you might decide to extend your activity to selling other things in your possession. You may be surprised to learn the value of items you have kept for many years, such as old toys, furnishings, etc. Just as you can simplify your coin collection for your heirs, you may find it worthwhile to simplify other possessions.

SPECIAL SECTION: FOR THE eBAY NOVICE

If you have not previously sold items via eBay, I recommend that you read a comprehensive guide on the subject. Though setting up an account is relatively easy, there are many considerations that are important. These include:

Payment. PayPal is the primary means of getting paid for your eBay sales. If you have not already done so, you will need to set up a PayPal account to receive and make payments. There are a variety of rules affecting how you receive payments from PayPal. One very important rule is that until you have established a long enough sales history, you may have to wait 21 days before you are allowed to withdraw funds you receive from your PayPal account. Another topic to research is the protections provided by PayPal to the buyer.

Shipping. eBay allows you to select from a variety of shipping options, and it also allows you as a seller to select to which markets your items will be available. In the United States, shipping is fairly straightforward and may either be at a fixed price you set or a calculated price based on weight. eBay provides USPS shipping labels at a discount that essentially offsets the fee on the shipping charge. This label also simplifies the actual shipping process.

International shipping is far more complicated. eBay offers a global shipping option whereby you ship to a U.S. address and the package is then shipped overseas by another party, but this can result in a very expensive shipping charge to your buyer. If you are going to ship overseas, you should take the time to explore the actual shipping costs for various countries and whether you might ship directly using eBay's shipping labels via the U.S. Postal Service.

Feedback. eBay encourages both buyer and seller to provide feedback on transactions, and it is the general ethic of eBay users to provide positive feedback should the transaction go smoothly. It is important that you participate by providing positive feedback to your customers and also operate in a manner such as to receive positive feedback yourself. It is not uncommon for quality sellers to have a positive feedback percentage between 99 and 100% over many transactions. Good communication with your customers, quick fulfillment, and honest representation of your items are the best ways to assure you receive positive feedback.

Feedback ratings ⓘ

★ ★ ★ ★ ★	162	Item as described	⊕ 206	⊖ 0	⊖ 0
★ ★ ★ ★ ★	185	Communication	Positive	Neutral	Negative
★ ★ ★ ★ ★	182	Shipping time			
★ ★ ★ ★ ★	163	Shipping charges		Feedback from the last 12 months	

Leaving and receiving good feedback will make your eBay experience go much smoother.

◆　◆　◆　◆　◆

Fees for participation. There are a variety of fees you pay for items you list and sell. Often it is possible to list your item for free (if you do not use special features), but when your item sells, eBay typically keeps 10%, and an additional 3% is charged by PayPal for payment processing. It is important that you factor these costs into your pricing.

The above are only a few of the considerations for selling via eBay. You should read a complete selling guide as well as familiarize yourself with eBay's online seller guides.

Though the focus of this book is clearly on coin collecting, most of the concepts and strategies included are applicable to any collectible.

CHAPTER 18

Other Collectibles

The central ideas of managing a valuable collection in retirement are:

Simplification. No matter what you have collected, you are in a much better position to consolidate and liquidate than your heirs. Doing so will produce the best return for your family and ease their burden.

Continued enjoyment. Adapt your collecting pursuits to take advantage of the differences in your situation as a retired collector. Utilize your additional time available to optimize your return and enjoyment.

Sell. Selling collectibles gives you experience that is helpful in acquiring other items at good prices. It also enables you to simplify your collection and acquire new items in a more cost-effective manner. Additionally, your proceeds will increase the funds available to you in general.

Allocate realistically. In deciding the ultimate disposition of your collection, consider the specific circumstances of your family with regard to both interest in your collection and financial needs, and develop a strategy that is optimal and fair.

Provide direction and guidance. Document what your family needs to know to simplify their ability to manage your collection and to avoid mistakes that will diminish the value they receive from it. You are in the best position to explain how the collection should be preserved and/or liquidated and under what circumstances. You are also able to provide the historical context for important items you would like them to preserve.

Resources. Become aware of the resources your family will need to deal with your collection, and document your recommendations. This could include recommended price guides and how these guides should be interpreted, as well as recommended venues for transactions.

Becoming familiar with some of the technological tools at coin collectors' disposal today can provide huge benefits.

CHAPTER 19

Technology

You may consider yourself "technology challenged," having gone through most of your adult life with minimal use of computers and easy access to support resources when you needed to use them. In today's day and age, however, you must attain some basic level of proficiency with technology to maximize your enjoyment of coin collecting. This chapter will provide some guidance on how to approach this challenge with a minimal expenditure of time and effort. It focuses on what you really need to know.

There are a plethora of "how-to" books intended to assist the reader with understanding their computer, but unfortunately, these works do not focus on the few essential lessons that are critical. As a result, a user may become familiar with many functions that are not essential and at the same time not fully understand the few most essential functions.

This section is not intended to serve as a comprehensive tutorial on using your computer. Its intent is to identify those tools that are essential and what skills you should take the time to learn to take advantage of them. One of the best ways to learn these skills is to have them demonstrated by a friend or family member who can then observe your efforts and guide you to an approach that works for you.

This section will also help prepare you to use coin-collecting resources on the Internet, which are extensive. The Internet provides you with the opportunity to connect with other hobbyists across the globe. The challenge is to do so in a manner that is both productive and safe.

The concepts addressed by this chapter apply to both Mac- and Windows-based computers and often to mobile devices as well.

ESSENTIAL KNOWLEDGE: PROGRAM AND FILE STORAGE

Many users do not take the time to understand the organization of programs and data on the computer. Such knowledge is essential.

All computers organize their programs and data in a hierarchical file system. The system is typically accessed through a browser. In Windows, the browser—technically called "File Explorer"—can be accessed via "My Computer" (XP), "Computer" (Vista, Windows 7, or Windows 8), or simply "File Explorer" (Windows 10) in the "Start" menu. On a Mac, the file browser is called "Finder."

Often, the first problem faced is finding out how to start the file system browser. On a Windows system, it is usually available by clicking on the Start button—which displays a panel with a list of programs that can be run—and then clicking on "Computer" or "My Computer." Note that clicking on the Start button will bring up a panel that displays two lists of programs; along the left are common applications that you use, and along the right are standard Windows functions, such as "Control Panel" and the aforementioned path to the file browser, "Computer."

Starting File Explorer via the Start menu in Windows.

Starting Finder on a Mac—the blue-and-gray icon appears at the far left of the application tray.

✦ ✦ ✦ ✦ ✦

On a Mac, you will usually find the Finder icon on the tray of applications. The leftmost (default location) icon on the application tray—a blue-and-gray smiling face—is the icon for Apple's Finder application, which is what you use to browse the system.

Once you start the file browser, you will immediately be confronted with the complexity of a computer. These browsers assume some basic familiarity with the organization of a computer, which you may not have. Conceptually, you are presented with lists of components of your computer on which files may be stored. This includes disk drives, CD drives, USB flash drives, Internet storage drives, and potentially other storage options as well. Sometimes they are clearly recognizable; for example, if you have one CD drive, the appearance of "CD Drive (E:)" would probably be clear. Sometimes, though, the listings are less intuitive. For example, "SanDisk (M:)" might be meaningless to you if you are unaware that the USB flash drive you have was manufactured by SanDisk.

In order to get past this complexity, there are several approaches you can pursue. The best approach would be to have someone show you how the browser works, providing sufficient detail so that you can become familiar with its most important functions. If you are courageous, you might take an experimental approach by following the exercises in a computer "how-to" guide on your own. Alternatively, you might attend a formal class.

When you take the time to become knowledgeable with regard to browsing your files, it is important that you write down what you have learned in case you need to jog your memory at some point in the future. Keep in mind that many computer novices do gain skills but then lose them over time if they are not used frequently enough.

The Windows File Explorer system browser, accessed via the "Computer" or "My Computer" option. The left-hand portion displays the components of your system in an expandable tree. "Desktop" is at the root. "Computer" starts the branch which contains all of the devices that are accessible to your computer (hard drives, CD drives, etc). The right-hand portion illustrates the contents of the item on the left that is currently selected.

❖ ❖ ❖ ❖ ❖

Computer file browsers usually allow you to view your files in either graphical form or textual lists. Textual lists are usually able to illustrate much more information at a time, but they are more complicated to interpret than graphical presentations. A common method of presentation of a hierarchical file system is a tree-like schematic in which each branch of the tree can be expanded to show more or less detail by clicking on a "+" or "–" sign or an arrow of some sort.

On a Mac, you will find a folder named Applications. If you open it, you will see all of the applications installed on your Mac. For example, Safari is the default Apple Web browser. On Windows, you will see a folder named Program Files. If you open it, you will see subfolders for many of your applications, often with recognizable names. Note, though that some Windows applications will install folders directly on the C: drive and have their own folder at the same level as Program Files.

Once you understand how to browse your system, you will want to become familiar with where your applications store data. For example, if you open a document or spreadsheet and click on Save As in the File menu, you will usually see the multi-level path that indicates where your actual document file is stored. You can confirm this location by starting the system browser, navigating to that folder, and locating your actual file.

One issue you may encounter is that of hidden files. Both Windows and Mac are programmed to set some types of files and folders as hidden from the user. For many users, that will be fine, but if you are unable to browse folders and receive access warnings, you may wish to toggle off this setting.

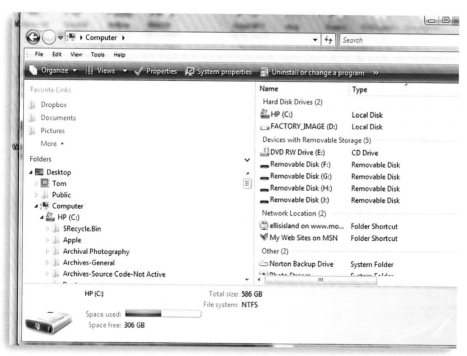

Here, clicking on "HP (C:)" along the left expands the tree so that the browser lists that drive's contents on the right. On this system, the "HP" indicates the particular computer is manufactured by Hewlett-Packard. The letter "C," followed by a colon, is usually assigned to the primary hard drive of the computer, which typically contains all of the primary folders accessible to Windows.

The illustration above shows a typical Finder window on a Mac.
In Mac's Finder, the left-hand side lists the primary components,
devices, and folders. In this illustration, the username has been selected,
showing variety of subfolders used by my various applications.

✦   ✦   ✦   ✦   ✦

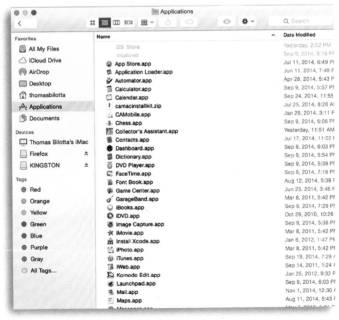

The Applications folder opened in Mac's Finder program.

Another important feature of Windows's File Explorer or the Mac's Finder is the ability to search for a file. If you know the name of the file, you can search for it, or if you know what type of file it is, you can perform a "wildcard" search for all files with the desired extension.

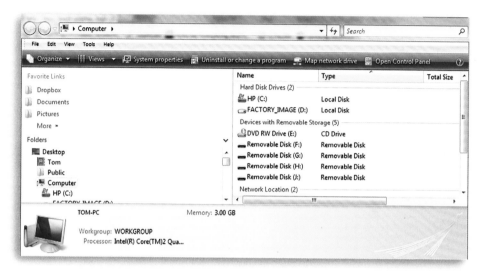

In Windows's File Explorer program, the search bar can be found in the upper-right-hand corner of the window.

✦ ✦ ✦ ✦ ✦

The user has initiated a search for a file named "testfile.doc." In this instance, no results have been found yet, so the message "Searching..." is displayed in the space where results would be shown.

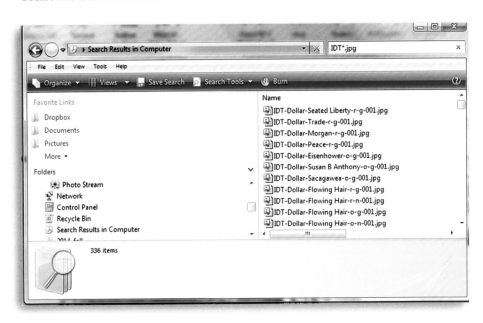

Instead of searching for a particular file, you can also search for all files containing certain strings in their names. Here, searching for "IDT*.jpg," will locate all files that start with "IDT" and end in .jpg.

❖ ❖ ❖ ❖ ❖

If you find the file you are looking for, you can right-click on it in the results list and then left-click on Properties. This will display a summary of information about the file, including the full location where it is stored (its path; highlighted here).

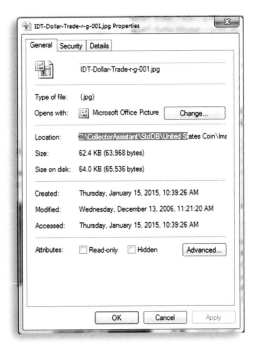

You will know when you have reached sufficient understanding of your system browser. The test is your ability to locate a file using the system browser if you know its location or name.

Your goal should not be to understand every aspect of the file system browser. Most important is that you know where your unique data is stored so that you can be sure to protect it. Your data consists of documents, pictures, and other files. Each application you use typically places your data in a particular folder. You need to take the time to learn where each application stores its files and confirm your ability to find them. You might create a document in a word-processing program, save it with a filename of "Test," and then search for it in your file system browser to locate the actual folder in which it is stored. Usually, when the file is found, the file browser will present the full folder hierarchy needed to reach it.

ESSENTIAL KNOWLEDGE: DATA BACKUP

The possibility of a problem with your hardware or software is very real. The most important strategy to avoid loss of your data is an effective backup approach.

Regular backup procedures are essential to protection of your data. I recommend a multifaceted strategy incorporating:

- Periodic full backups, always using new media storage devices not permanently incorporated in your computer
- Periodic partial backups to removable media such as USB flash drives and, in some instances, to network or local drives
- Automated Internet backups (optional)

Whatever backup media you select, you should use the system-browsing skills you've developed to locate your actual backup files, understand their nature, and review recovery procedures.

Using new media devices for each backup is the surest way to assure you will never suffer a total data loss. Though overwriting backups is a common approach and saves you money on new storage devices, these devices are inexpensive in the first place. Also, the practice of overwriting backups suffers from a fundamental problem in that some users are not instantly aware of a data loss, and thus might replace an older backup from which data could be recovered with a newer set of files that actually has already been affected by data loss, unbeknownst to the user.

Another common flawed approach is to sign up for an automated Internet backup service and assume that your data is automatically protected. This approach leaves many unanswered questions:

- How can you be sure the files you need are actually being backed up?
- How often are older backups overwritten, and for how long may an older backup be accessed?
- What are the procedures to recover a file when data is lost, and how can it be done with minimal impact on current data?
- Does your backup guard against all risks, including loss of data and backup media in a theft or fire?

ESSENTIAL KNOWLEDGE: SAFE USE OF EMAIL

Email is a vital link to other coin-collecting resources throughout the world. It is vital, though, that you use this communication medium in a safe manner.

Email is one of the most commonly used means of intrusion into your computer system and files, as anyone can send you email once they obtain your email address. A common approach is to send you an email which appears to be from an individual or company with which you do business and includes a link to update some account information. In fact, the link is often to a fraudulent site intended to look like the real site of the entity you do business with. If you do enter login information using this fraudulent site, you may release that confidential information to an individual or organization that will use it to log into the real site under your account and commit identity theft.

It is very easy to mimic the appearance of a business by taking screen captures of their Web site, logos, etc. It is also very easy to avoid falling victim to this attack, which is commonly referred to as "phishing."

The most important rule is that you avoid clicking on links in an email unless you are absolutely certain the message is from a trusted source. Email links should never be used to log into a financial account (or other account containing similar personal information). Always enter the URL of the company you are trying to reach directly into the navigation bar of your browser so that you are certain you are at the company's legitimate Web site. Many such sites also incorporate a two-step login including a picture or phrase which appears after you enter your login name. The correct appearance of the phrase or image is a confirmation that you are indeed at the correct site.

Note also that links in emails (and elsewhere on the Web) can be deceptive in that the text that is hyperlinked does not necessarily have anything to do with the page to which it is linked. This is something that is not understood by some computer users. The actual link is stored elsewhere and associated with some text and/or pictures that you see by HTML coding. As the text and/or images that you see and click on are defined separately from the link, the two may be completely unrelated.

Warning: do not even right-click on links that are not from trusted sources, as a slip of the hand may result in actually clicking on the link.

If you do receive a link from a trusted source, right-click on the link, left-click on Properties (in Windows), note the exact URL, and make sure it is consistent with your expectations. Many phony links will contain paths intended to mimic the real site, but the phony link will contain a different top-level domain name, such as that of a different country.

An email containing a link. Note that the hyperlinked text reads "This is a really neat site." See next page for more images.

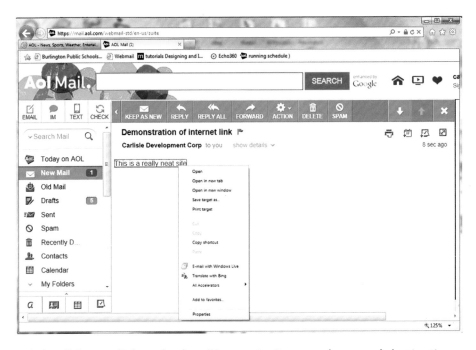

Right-click on a link and select "Properties" to see the actual destination, which may not be related to the text that is linked.

* * * * *

In this instance, the hyperlinked text did not specify what the URL of the destination site is. Until you know the destination, do not click on a suspicious link.

ESSENTIAL KNOWLEDGE:
ATTACHING FILES IN EMAIL

All email systems allow users to attach a file to be sent along with an email. However, many users do not take the time to learn how to send attached files along with an email. This function can be used to share pictures and other data with other collectors. For example, you may wish to send an image of one of your coins to a dealer or collector.

Though the specific process is different on each email system (AOL, Gmail, Outlook, etc.), the procedure is similar:

1. Address a new email to the desired party
2. Click on a button labeled "Attach" or "Attach File" or an icon indicating attachment, such as a paper clip
3. A file browser will be displayed so you can navigate to the folder containing the file to be attached
4. Select the file and send the email

Some email systems limit the size and types of files that can be attached. A common size for the maximum of a file attachment is 10 MB (megabytes). Some systems will not allow application files (which end with extensions such as .exe, .app, and .dll) to be emailed. In these instances, you may need to place your files in a compressed container file (frequently a .zip extension), which will reduce its size.

The steps in sending an attachment are fairly straightforward. You start by preparing a normal email, filling in the address, subject line, and body of the email. In the example pictured on the next page, the user is sending a friend (person@aol.com) a copy of a picture recently taken.

Clicking on the paper-clip icon at the left of the toolbar opens a file browser that can be used to locate the file to be attached. In this instance, the file is on the Desktop. Click on the file to highlight it and then click on Open or OK.

This takes us back to the email, where the names of any attached files now appear just below the subject line. The email is now ready to send.

The specific buttons and steps differ slightly on each email interface, but the basics are the same. You address a normal email and, when ready to attach file(s), click on the button or icon supplied for this purpose. A system browser will appear, which you use to navigate to the file and select it for attachment.

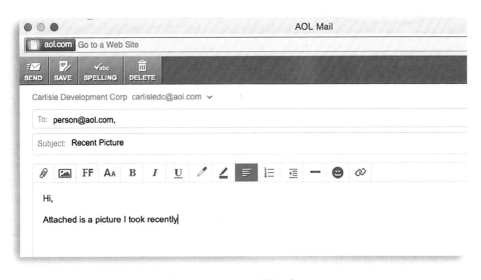

Prepare to send an attachment via email by first starting a new message, addressing it to the recipient, and adding a subject and body text.

* * * * *

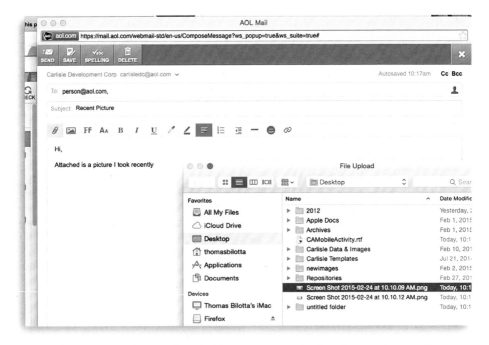

Select an attachment by clicking your email client's attachment icon (likely a paper clip) and finding the file within your computer's file browser.

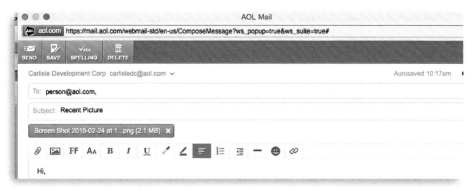

This email has a file attached and is ready to send.

✦ ✦ ✦ ✦ ✦

ESSENTIAL KNOWLEDGE: INTERNET BROWSING SAFETY

It is very likely that you will encounter Web sites that threaten your computer and data, and these Web sites may not look any different than safe Web sites you use frequently. There are several important aspects to safe Web browsing. For sites containing financial or other sensitive data, make sure to enter the URL correctly. Once you have done so, you may want to bookmark the site so that you can return there easily. There are many fraudulent sites that mimic real sites' URLs by using common misspellings of the real sites' URLs. When in doubt, close the browser window, open a new one and retype the site URL.

In general, do not click on links on sites with which you are not familiar. Also, be aware of when you are leaving a trusted site. For example, you may be browsing the site of a company with which you do business. Most links are probably to other pages of the trusted site. Some links, however, may take you to partner or external sites. In some cases, you will receive a warning so that you are aware you are leaving the trusted site.

Be wary of any Web site that trips your Web browser's security warnings.

ESSENTIAL KNOWLEDGE: MAC VERSUS WINDOWS

There are advocates of both Macs and Windows-based PCs as the best choice for an easy user experience. The truth is that both systems are very similar with regard to the essential items described above.

The reasons a user purchases and uses one over the other usually have to do with factors other than usability. Windows-based PCs are usually significantly less expensive for comparable performance. Macs are usually easier to get started on, primarily because the hardware is totally controlled by Apple.

Security threats are much more prevalent with Windows-based computers primarily due to their much larger market share and the fact they have been considered less "cool" than Macs.

Whichever you choose, productive use and protection of your data requires you to gain the essential knowledge outlined in this chapter.

ESSENTIAL KNOWLEDGE: MONITOR RESOLUTION

Some retired coin collectors may suffer from diminished eyesight. Fortunately, an appropriately sized monitor supported by the right graphics card can provide good visibility for almost anyone. Most computers allow you to adjust the size of text (fonts) and the resolution of your display. The larger your monitor is and the more resolution choices your display has, the more options you will enjoy.

Generally, setting your display at higher resolution will present more data (pixels per inch), but elements on the screen will also appear smaller. The best approach is to set your display at the highest resolution at which you can read text comfortably. This will ensure comfortable reading with presentation of the maximum amount of data. Adjusting the resolution of your display is usually accomplished by right-clicking on the Desktop and selecting either Display Options or Screen Resolution (Windows) or in System Preferences (Mac), and the text size can normally be changed within an individual program (word-processing software like Microsoft Word and Internet browsers such as Internet Explorer, Google Chrome, and Mozilla Firefox all offer this option).

If you know you have poor eyesight, make sure to purchase a large monitor (20 inches, measured diagonally, or larger). Monitors have become significantly less expensive in recent years, and larger monitors are also lighter in weight thanks to LCD technology.

In Windows 7, you can access Screen Resolution options by right-clicking on the Desktop and clicking on "Personalize."

Conclusion

As it has for many collectors, your pursuit of coin collecting has provided significant enjoyment as you have earned a living and perhaps raised a family. With proper planning, the results of this effort can benefit your family for many years and provide them with a lifelong memento.

Inadequate preparation, however, can result in loss of value, conflict among your heirs, and/or the burdens of difficult and unenjoyable tasks for your loved ones. Your goal should be to ensure the most positive outcome of your collecting pursuits.

A small amount of planning and preparation goes a long way to meeting this objective. After many years of collecting, there is no more productive use of your time spent on the hobby than organizing your collection for its eventual disposition. This task can be viewed as a challenging one that expands your experience in numismatics and introduces you to new facets with which you have little or no experience.

You may have deferred selling any parts of your collection many times in the past due to unwillingness to make a commitment to sell coins you have accumulated over the years. This inaction needs to be overcome by your desire to take care of your family, and this motivation should be supported by your knowledge of reality. The truth is that many coins in your collection are not actually of much personal significance, and liquidating these items will benefit your collecting efforts as well as your heirs. If you are having difficulty making the decision to sell, ask yourself what makes an item special (and therefore something that you cannot part with), and be honest with the answer. For example, if you can readily replace the item by purchasing an identical coin through a large number of venues (online stores, mail-order dealers, etc.), then it is likely not very special.

Focus on the significant coins and related collectibles, keep your family and your own best interests in mind, and plan wisely for the future. Most of all, continue to enjoy your hobby in retirement!

Appendix A

Grading Coins:
A Primer for Inheritors

This introductory guide is adapted from Q. David Bowers's Grading Coins by Photographs, Second Edition.

HOW TO USE THIS APPENDIX

The following pages cover the grading parameters for several popularly collected U.S. coin series.

To grade a coin, particularly at the circulated levels, match it to a picture within its series' section (using the tips under "Viewing Coins for Grading" that follows this section). Then read the description. Keep in mind that opinions differ, and within a given type there can be differences as well. One rule does not fit all. However, general rules are useful, and you should be able to do quite well, given some practice.

The photographs shown are of actual coins in the marketplace, the majority of them attributed by PCGS and NGC. There are no composite photographs. In each case the obverse and reverse illustrations are from the same specimen. While a picture is worth a thousand words, so they say, the text has value as well. Each picture is accompanied by an explanation, sometimes a little narrative, which you may find useful. To get an even broader view, it may help to go on the Internet and seek out similar coins in similar grades from the leading services; that way you can verify what is shown here and also get some ideas as to differences that can occur within a given grade. You can also do this sort of "field" work by visiting coin shops and shows.

It is important for you as an evaluator to grade to a fixed standard, such as by the guidelines outlined here, and then endeavor to relate coins in the marketplace to these standards. Otherwise, you might see a dozen overgraded coins marked "EF-40" and assume that the coins are right and that the standards are wrong.

In the following pages each section has an introduction giving a thumb-nail history, plus, and especially important, what to look for in sharp striking. While it can be argued that sharpness of strike is one thing and grade is another, both combine in real life to make a given coin desirable or undesirable. Grade alone will not do it. Accordingly, reading these guidelines is strongly suggested.

You would do well to remember that there is quality within every grade. Not all EF-45, MS-65, or other-grade coins are equal. There will be high-end coins within every grade as well as midrange and low-end pieces. In certain instances, a collector might find a high-end MS-64 coin to be a better purchase than a low-end MS-66.

VIEWING COINS FOR GRADING

For the proper grading of coins a good source of illumination and a good magnifier are both needed. The best lighting is an incandescent light-bulb of, say, 60 watts, placed within a foot or two of a coin. The surrounding room should not be brightly lighted. Halogen lamps are used by some, but there have been warnings that they can be dangerous. As coins such as Proofs might reflect light into your eyes, you may want to avoid using this type of lamp, but they are in wide use at conventions and in coin shops. Finally, fluorescent lamps are not recommended, but they are often used as well.

To examine a coin, a handheld magnifier is desirable. A level of magnification such as 4x, which can be doubled with a similar lens to be 8x, is ideal for most coins. A loupe giving higher magnification is desirable if details need to be checked. However, the narrower the field of vision and the higher the magnification, the more difficult it is to grade a coin, as you can literally get too close to the subject. (A microscope would be virtually useless.)

Take a coin and hold it by its edges, or by the edges of its container. Rotate it slowly, reflecting the light from the lamp to the surface of the coin, into your eye, at first without the use of a magnifier, to form an initial opinion of the grade. Then use a magnifying glass. This procedure will highlight the field and surfaces and will make hairlines and marks evident. You will quickly see that lines can appear and reappear as the coin is turned, depending on the orientation to the light. A tiny scratch viewed parallel to the light beam might become invisible, while if it is crosswise to the light beam it will be fully seen. Do this carefully as you view both sides of a coin. The edge, sometimes called the "third side" of a coin, should be checked as well, assuming the coin is not in a sealed holder.

Grading coins in a location with distant overhead lights or table lamps can be misleading, as coins often appear to be nicer than they actually are. For proper grading, a coin needs to be observed close up, and carefully.

Many "slabs" (plastic encapsulation cases) holding certified coins have become scuffed or have tiny lines and marks of their own. If you wiggle a slab slightly, any marks on the slab will move in relation to the coin inside. In contrast, hairlines or marks on the coin itself will not move.

INDIAN HEAD CENTS (1859–1909)

History. After nearly a dozen varieties of patterns were made in 1858, in 1859 the Indian Head was adopted as the new motif for the cent. Observers of the time noted the incongruity of placing a Native American war bonnet on a bust which was meant to be both female and classically Greek; designer James B. Longacre's earlier use of a feathered tiara on the Indian Head three-dollar gold piece had been viewed as less strange. The reverse of the 1859 coin illustrates an olive (or laurel) wreath. In 1860 this was changed to a wreath of oak and other leaves with a shield at the apex, a design continued through the end of the series in 1909. From 1859 through spring 1864 cents were struck in copper-nickel, the alloy used earlier for Flying Eagle cents. In 1864 a new bronze alloy was adopted.

Indian Head cents remained in circulation through the 1940s, but by the early 1950s were rarely seen. In the 1930s, when Whitman and other coin boards and folders became widely available, collectors picked many key dates out of circulation. The typical grade for the scarce issues of the 1870s was Good or so, and the 1908-S and 1909-S could be found in VF.

Striking and Sharpness. The strike on Indian Head cents can vary widely. On the obverse the points to check include the details at the tips of the feathers and the diamonds on the ribbon. The diamonds cannot be used as a grading marker, and the feather tips can be used only if you have familiarity with how sharp the coin was struck to begin with. In general, the reverse is usually sharper, but check the leaf and shield details. On many bronze cents beginning in the 1870s the bottom of the N of ONE and the tops of the EN of CENT are light, as they were in the dies (this is not factored when grading). Check the denticles on both sides. Gener-

ally, copper-nickel cents of the early 1860s are candidates for light striking as are later issues in the bronze format, of the 1890s onward.

Availability. In worn grades Indian Head cents are available in proportion
to their mintages, in combination with survival rates being higher for the
later issues. (The low-mintage 1909-S was saved in larger quantities than
the higher-mintage 1877, as an example.) MS coins survive as a matter of
chance, with those of 1878 and before being much scarcer than those of
1879 and later, and some of the 1900s being readily available. Many if not
most higher-grade MS coins have been dipped or recolored, unless they
are a warm orange-red color with traces of natural brown. The search for
quality among bronze cents is particularly challenging. Some tiny toning
flecks are to be expected on many coins, and as long as they are microscopic they can often be ignored (except in grades on the far side of
MS-65). A set of MS-65 coins in RB or RD can be formed quickly, but a
collection with original color, sharp strike, and excellent eye appeal may
take several years.

During the years these coins were in production, collectors who wanted
single pieces each year often bought Proofs. In the late 1930s, many
1878–1909 Proof Indian Head cents began to be released from several
estate hoards. These had vivid violet and blue iridescent toning from
being stored for decades in tissue paper. They are highly sought-after
today.

Proofs. Proof Indian Head cents were made of all dates 1859 to 1909.
The 1864 bronze variety with a tiny L (for designer James B. Longacre)
on the ribbon is a rarity, with only about two dozen known. Generally,
Proofs are sharp strikes until the 1890s, when some can be weak. On
bronze coins tiny carbon flecks are typical, but should be microscopic. If
larger, avoid, and at PF-65 or higher, avoid as well. The majority of Proofs
have been dipped, and many bronze pieces have been retoned. Most
undipped coins are either rich brown (can be very attractive) or red and
brown. The late John J. Pittman spent 50 years trying to find a Gem Proof
1907 Indian Head cent with brilliant original color! Cherrypicking is the
order of the day. Extra value can be found in BN and RB, simply because
investors won't buy them; instead, they are drawn to RD coins, most of
which have been "improved" (dipped and retoned).

Proofs are generally designated BN if the surfaces are mainly brown or
iridescent, or have up to perhaps 30% original mint red-orange color
(there is little consistency, within the hobby community, in this determi-

nation). RB is the designation if the surface is a mixture of red-orange and brown, best if blended together nicely, but often with patches of mint color among brown areas. RD designates a coin with original (in theory) mint-red orange, always blending to slight natural brown toning unless the coin has been dipped. Likely, any RD coin with even a few hairlines has been cleaned (or at least mishandled) at one time; in most such cases, what appears to be mint-red color is not original. Certification services take no notice of this. For this reason, a connoisseur will prefer a gem BN coin with no hairlines to a PF-65 or 66 RD coin with some hairlines. Proof copper-nickel Indian Head cents of 1859 to 1864 need no letter to indicate color, as their hue derives more from the nickel than the copper. As a general rule, these survive in higher grades and with greater eye appeal, as they stayed "brilliant" (the watchword for most collectors until recent decades) and did not need dipping. Moreover, when such pieces were cleaned and acquired hairlines, they tended to be fewer than on a bronze coin, due to the very hard nature of the copper-nickel alloy.

GRADING STANDARDS

MS-60 to 70 (Mint State). *Obverse:* Contact marks, most obvious in the field, are evident at MS-60, diminishing at MS-61, 62, and higher. This abrasion is most noticeable on copper-nickel cents, for it blends in with the background on bronze issues. The cheek of the Indian and the field

1894. Graded MS-66+RD.

show some evidence as well. Typical color is BN, occasionally RB at MS-63 and 64, unless dipped to be RD. At gem MS-65 or finer there is no trace of abrasion. A few tiny nicks or marks may be seen, but none are obvious. At MS-67 and finer the coin will approach perfection. Check "RD" coins for originality. A theoretically perfect MS-70 will have no marks at all, even under a strong magnifier. Although in practice this is not always consistent, at MS-66 and higher there should be no staining or other problems, and the coin should have good eye appeal overall. *Reverse:* Check the high parts of the wreath for abrasion. Otherwise the above comments apply.

Illustrated coin: Absolutely unblemished, this lovely gem retains every bit of its original, reddish-orange mint color and frosty texture.

AU-50, 53, 55, 58 (About Uncirculated).
Obverse: At AU-50, wear is most noticeable on the hair above the ear, on the
central portion of the ribbon, on the curl
to the right of the ribbon, and near the
feather tips, although the last is not a reliable indicator due to striking. Luster is
present, but mostly in protected areas. At

1873, Close 3, with doubled
LIBERTY. Graded AU-50.

AU-53 and 55, wear is less. At AU-58 friction is evident, rather than actual
wear. Luster, toned brown, is nearly complete at AU-58, but may be
incomplete in the field. *Reverse:* At AU-50, light wear is seen on the ribbon and the higher-relief areas of the leaves, while the lower areas retain
their detail. Some luster may be present in protected areas. At AU-53 and
55, wear is less and luster is more extensive. An AU-58 coin will have
nearly full luster and show only light friction.

Illustrated coin: This is a coin with excellent eye appeal. Its glossy brown
surfaces retain some luster.

EF-40, 45 (Extremely Fine). *Obverse:* Wear
is more extensive, but all of LIBERTY is
very clear. Wear is seen on the hair above
and below the ear, on the central portion
of the ribbon, and on the feather tips.
Overall the coin is bold. Scattered marks
are normal for this and lower grades, most

1869. Graded EF-45.

often seen on the cheek and in the field. *Reverse:* The higher-relief parts
of the leaves and ribbon bow show light wear, but details are sharp in
lower areas. Some tiny lines in the vertical stripes in the shield may be
blended. Scattered marks may be present, but on all grades they are usually fewer on the reverse than on the obverse.

VF-20, 30 (Very Fine). *Obverse:* Wear is
more extensive. LIBERTY shows significant wear on BE but is sharp overall. Most
hair detail is gone. The feather tips show
greater wear (the extent of which will
depend on the original strike). The ribbon and hair no longer show separation.

1877. Graded VF-30.

Reverse: Wear is more extensive than on the preceding, and many tiny
vertical lines are fused together. Detail is still good on lower levels of the
leaves.

Illustrated coin: Note the slight granularity to the surfaces.

F-12, 15 (Fine). *Obverse:* By tradition the word LIBERTY should be fully readable, but weak on the higher letters of LIB. PCGS suggests this is true except if a coin was lightly struck. Full or incomplete, well struck or lightly struck, no matter what the coin, most buyers still want the word to be discernible. Other areas have correspondingly more wear than on the next-higher grade. *Reverse:* The higher areas of the leaves and the bow show wear. The shield shows greater wear than on the preceding. Overall, the reverse appears to be less worn than the obverse, this being generally true of all circulated grades.

1909-S. Graded F-12.

VG-8, 10 (Very Good). *Obverse:* A total of at least three letters in LIBERTY must be visible. This can be a combination of several partial letters. PCGS does not adhere to this rule and suggests that wear on the feathers is a better indicator. The rim may blend into the field in areas, depending on striking. *Reverse:* Wear is even more extensive. Leaves on the left have hardly any detail, while those on the right may have limited detail. The rim is complete.

1877. Graded VG-8.

Illustrated coin: The weakness at the base of the N of ONE is due to the nature of the dies, not to wear.

G-4, 6 (Good). *Obverse:* The coin is worn flat, with the portrait visible mostly in outline form, with only slight indication of feathers. Lettering and date are complete. Part of the rim is usually gone. At G-6, the rim is clearer. *Reverse:* The wreath is nearly flat, although some hints of detail may be seen on the right side. All letters are readable, although the inscription is light at the center (on issues from the 1870s onward). The rim is discernible all around, but is light in areas. At G-6 the rim is clearly delineated.

1877. Graded G-4 or slightly better.

Illustrated coin: This is a "strong" Good, a candidate for G-6 (not an official ANA grade, but widely used), with excellent definition within that grade. The weakness at the base of the N of ONE is due to the nature of the dies, not to wear.

AG-3 (About Good). *Obverse:* Most letters are worn away, as is the rim. The portrait is in outline form. The date is clearly readable, but may be weak or missing at the bottom. *Reverse:* Extensive wear prevails, although the rim will usually be more discernible than on the obverse. Most lettering, or sometimes all, is readable.

1877. Graded AG-3.

 Illustrated coin: As is often the case, the reverse, if evaluated separately, could be graded G-4. Some light spotting is acceptable.

PF-60 to 70 (Proof). *Obverse and Reverse:* Gem PF-65 coins will have very few hairlines, and these are visible only under a strong magnifying glass. At any level and color, a Proof with hairlines likely (though not necessarily) has been cleaned. At PF-67 or higher there should be no evidence of hairlines or friction at all. Such

1864, Copper-Nickel. Graded PF-66.

a coin is fully original. PF-60 coins can be dull from repeated dipping and cleaning and are often toned iridescent colors. At PF-63 the mirrorlike fields should be attractive, and hairlines should be minimal. These are easiest to see when the coin is held at an angle to the light. No rubbing is seen. PF-64 coins are even nicer.

LINCOLN, WHEAT EARS REVERSE, CENTS (1909–1958)

History. The Lincoln cent debuted in 1909 in honor of the hundredth anniversary of the birth of Abraham Lincoln. Sculptor and engraver Victor David had been chosen to design the new cent because the artistry of Chief Engraver Charles Barber was under heavy criticism at the time. The new cent was released on August 2, 1909, and the earliest coins of the year's issue had Brenner's initials (V.D.B.) on the reverse; this was soon discontinued. (His initials would be restored in 1918, on the obverse, on Lincoln's shoulder.) This was the first U.S. cent to feature the motto IN GOD WE TRUST.

 From 1909 to 1942 the coins were struck in bronze. In 1943, during World War II, zinc-coated steel was used for their planchets, as a way to reserve copper for the war effort. The bronze alloy would be resumed in 1944. (Although no bronze cents were officially issued in 1943, a few pieces struck on bronze or silver planchets are known to exist for that year; bronze examples have recently sold for more than $200,000. Such errors presumably occur when an older planchet is mixed in with the normal supply of planchets and goes through the minting process. Through a similar production error, a few 1944 cents were struck on steel planchets. Beware the many regular steel cents of 1943 that were later plated with copper, either as novelties or to deceive collectors; a magnet will reveal their true nature.) In 1944, 1945, and 1946, the Mint used salvaged gun-cartridge cases as its source metal for coining cents. In Mint State, the color of cents of these years can appear slightly different from other bronze Wheat Ear cents.

The Philadelphia, Denver, and San Francisco mints all produced Lincoln Wheat Ear cents, but not in all years. The Wheat Ears reverse design was used from 1909 until the coin's 50th anniversary in 1959, at which time it was replaced with a view of the Lincoln Memorial.

Striking and Sharpness. As a rule, Lincoln cents of 1909 through 1914 are fairly well struck. From 1915 through the end of the 1920s, many are weak, with Denver Mint coins particularly so. Issues of the 1930s onward are mostly well struck. With many different die pairs used over a long period of time, striking quality varies. On the obverse, check for details in Lincoln's hair and beard. Also check the lettering and the inner edge of the rim. Tiny marks on the shoulder of Lincoln indicate a weak strike there; this area cannot be used to determine wear on high-grade coins. (During striking, there was not enough die pressure to fill this, the deepest point of the obverse die; therefore, stray marks on the raw planchet remain evident in this spot.) On the reverse check the wheat stalks, letters, and inner rim. A weak strike will usually manifest itself on the O of ONE (the area directly opposite Lincoln's shoulder). Coins struck from overused or "tired" dies can have grainy or even slightly wavy fields on either side.

Availability. Of the earlier Lincoln Wheat Ears cents, those of 1909 are easily found in MS; later early dates are scarcer, although Philadelphia varieties were made in higher quantities and are more often seen. Beginning in the early 1930s, collectors saved bank-wrapped rolls of Mint State cents in large quantities (starting mainly in 1934, though the low-mintage 1931-S was also hoarded). Dates after this time all are plentiful, although some more so than others, and there are a number of scarce and rare varieties. The collector demand for scarcer Lincoln cents and higher-grade issues is intense, resulting in a strong market. Many Mint State coins before the 1930s have been dipped and recolored, this being particularly true of pieces listed as RD. Others are stained and blotchy.

Proofs. Matte Proof Lincoln cents of a new style were made from 1909 to 1916. These have minutely matte or pebbled surfaces caused by special treatment of the dies. The rims are square and sharp. Such pieces cannot easily be told from certain circulation strikes with similar borders. Certified holders usually list these simply as "Proof," not "Matte Proof." Buy only coins that have been verified by an expert. Most are brown, or brown with tinges of red. Nearly all full "red" coins have been dipped or recolored.

Exceptional specimens dated 1917 are reported to exist, although no records exist to indicate they are true Proofs.

Mirror-finish Proofs were made from 1936 to 1942 and again from 1950 to 1958. Proofs of this era are mostly from dies polished overall (including the portrait), although some later issues have frosted ("cameo") portraits. Quality can be a problem for the 1936 to 1942 issues. Check for carbon spots and recoloring. Proofs of later dates are easy to find.

Generally, Proofs below 63 are unattractive and are not desired by most collectors.

GRADING STANDARDS

MS-60 to 70 (Mint State). *Obverse and Reverse:* At MS-65 and higher, the luster is rich on all areas, except perhaps the shoulder (which may be grainy and show original planchet surface). There is no rubbing, and no contact marks are visible except under magnification. Coins with

1943. Graded MS-68.

full or nearly full mint orange-red color can be designated RD; those with full or nearly full brown-toned surfaces can be designated BN; and those with a substantial percentage of red-orange and of brown can be called RB. Ideally, MS-65 or finer coins should have good eye appeal, which in the RB category means nicely blended colors, not stained or blotched. Below MS-65, full RD coins become scarce, and at MS-60 to 62 are virtually non-existent, unless they have been dipped. Copper is a very active metal, and influences such as slight abrasions, contact marks, and so on that define the grade also affect the color. The ANA grading standards allow for "dull" and/or "spotted" coins at MS-60 and 61, as well as incomplete luster. In the marketplace, interpretations often vary widely. BN and RB coins at MS-60 and 61 are apt to be more attractive than (dipped) RD coins.

Illustrated coin: This zinc-coated steel cent is an ultra gem in quality.

AU-50, 53, 55, 58 (About Uncirculated). *Obverse:* Slight wear shows on Lincoln's cheekbone to the left of his nose, and also on his beard. At AU-55 or 58 there may be some hints of mint red-orange. Most coins in About Uncirculated are BN, but are often not designated by color. *Reverse:* Slight wear is evident on the stalks of wheat to the left and right. Otherwise, the same standards apply as for the obverse.

1909-S, V.D.B. Graded AU-50BN.

   Illustrated coin: This is a sharp example of the most famous Lincoln cent issue.

EF-40, 45 (Extremely Fine). *Obverse:* Light wear is seen on Lincoln's portrait, and hair detail is gone on the higher areas, especially above the ear. *Reverse:* Light wear is seen overall, but the parallel lines in the wheat stalks are clearly separated.

1909, No V.D.B. Graded EF-45.

VF-20, 30 (Very Fine). *Obverse:* Lincoln's portrait is worn all over, with most hair detail gone at the center. Hair separation is seen at the back and the top of the head, but hairs are blended together. The jaw outline is clear. The center of the ear is defined and the bowtie is clear. The date and lettering is sharp. *Reverse:* More wear is seen, but still the lines in the wheat stalks are separated. Lettering shows wear but is very clear.

1909-S, V.D.B. Graded VF-20.

   Illustrated coin: Some gray discoloration is hardly noticeable near the rims.

F-12, 15 (Fine). *Obverse:* More wear is seen overall. Hair definition is less. The center of the ear is partially visible. The jaw outline and bowtie are clear. *Reverse:* Most lines in the wheat stalks are either weak or blended with others, but more than half of the separating lines are clear.

1914-D. Graded F-12.

VG-8, 10 (Very Good). *Obverse:* The portrait is more worn, with only slight hair strands visible (thick strands blended). The ear opening is visible. The bowtie and jacket show fewer details. *Reverse:* The lines in the wheat stalks are blended together in flat areas. Perhaps 40% to 50% of the separating lines can be seen. The rim may be weak in areas.

1910-S. Graded VG-8.

G-4, 6 (Good). *Obverse:* The portrait is well worn. Some slight details are seen at the top of the head and the bottom of the coat. LIBERTY is weak. The rim may touch or blend with the tops of the letters forming IN GOD WE TRUST. The date and mintmark (if any) are very clear. *Reverse:* The wheat stalks are flat, with just a few scattered details visible.

1911. Graded G-4.

AG-3 (About Good). *Obverse:* Wear is extensive. The portrait is mostly in outline form, with only scattered details visible. LIBERTY is weak and perhaps with some letters missing. IN GOD WE TRUST blends in with the rim, and several letters are very weak or missing. *Reverse:* The rim is worn down to blend with the outside of the wheat stalks in some areas, although some hints of the edge of the stalks can be seen. Lettering is weak, with up to several letters missing.

1913-D. Graded AG-3.

PF-60 to 70 (Matte Proof). *Obverse and Reverse:* At the Matte PF-65 level or higher there are no traces of abrasion or contact marks. Color will range from brown (BN)—the most common—to brown with significant tinges of mint red-orange (RB), or with much mint color (RD). Most RD coins have been dipped. Some tiny flecks are normal on coins certified as PF-65 but should be microscopic or absent above that. Coins in the PF-60 to 63 range are BN or sometimes RB—almost impossible to be RD unless dipped. Lower-grade Proofs usually have poor eye appeal.

1912, Matte Proof.
Graded PF-64RD.

Illustrated coin: This lovely coin has above-average eye appeal.

PF-60 to 70 (Mirror Proof). *Obverse and Reverse:* PF-65 and higher coins are usually RB (colors should be nicely blended) or RD, the latter with bright red-orange fading slightly to hints of brown. Some tiny flecks are normal on coins certified as PF-65 but should be microscopic or absent above that. PF-60 and 61 coins can be

1936, Mirror Proof.
Graded PF-65RD.

dull, stained, or spotted but still have some original mint color. Coins with fingerprints must be given a low numerical grade. Lower-grade Proofs usually have poor eye appeal.

Illustrated coin: A few flecks are seen here and there.

INDIAN HEAD OR BUFFALO NICKELS (1913–1938)

History. The Indian Head nickel five-cent piece today is almost universally known as the "Buffalo" nickel, after the American bison on the reverse. The design made its debut in 1913. James Earle Fraser, a sculptor well known in the private sector, was its creator. The obverse features an authentic portrait of a Native American, modeled as a composite from life, with three subjects posing. Unlike any preceding coin made for circulation, the Buffalo nickel had little in the way of open, smooth field surfaces. Instead, most areas on the obverse and reverse were filled with design elements or, especially on the reverse, an irregular background, as on a bas-relief plaque. Soon after the first coins were released, it was thought that the inscription FIVE CENTS, on a high area of the motif, would wear too quickly. The Mint modified the design to lower the ground under the bison, which had been arranged in the form of a mound (on what became known as Variety 1). The flat-ground design is called Variety 2.

Striking and Sharpness. Most circulation-strike Buffalo nickels are poorly struck in one or more areas, and for many Denver and San Francisco issues of the 1920s the striking is very poor. However, enough sharp strikes exist among common dates of the 1930s that one can be found with some patience. Certification services do not reflect the quality of strike on their labels, so examine carefully. The matter of striking sharpness on Buffalo nickels is an exceedingly important aspect for the connoisseur (who might prefer, for example, a sharply struck coin in AU-58 over a fully lustrous MS example with much shallower detail). Points to check on the obverse include the center of the coin, especially the area immediately above the tie on the braid. On the reverse check the fur on the head of the bison, and the fur "line" above the bison's shoulder on its back. On both sides, examine the overall striking of letters and other details.

Availability. Among circulated varieties of standard dates and mintmarks, availability is in proportion to their mintages. Among early issues the 1913-S, Variety 2, is the scarcest. The date wore away more quickly on the Variety 1 coins than on the modified design used from later 1913 through the end of the series. In the 1920s the 1926-S is the hardest to find. Collectors sought Buffalo nickels from circulation until the 1960s, after which most were gone. By that time the dates in the teens were apt to have their dates completely worn away, or be AG-3 or G-4. Among MS nickels, the issues of 1913 were saved in quantity as novelties, although 1913-S, Variety 2, is slightly scarce. Philadelphia Mint issues are readily available through the 1920s, while MS-63 and finer mintmarked issues from 1914 to 1927 can range from scarce to rare. From 1931 to 1938, all dates and mintmarks were saved in roll quantities, and all are plentiful today. Many Buffalo nickels in MS are very rare if with Full Details, this being especially true for mintmarked issues after 1913, into the early 1930s. Sharpness of strike is not noted on certification holders, but a connoisseur would probably rather own a Full Details coin in MS-65 than an MS-66 or higher with a flat strike.

Proofs. Proof Buffalo nickels are of two main styles. Matte Proofs were made from 1913 to 1916 and are rare. These have minutely granular or matte surfaces, are sharply struck with Full Details of the design on both sides, and have edges (as viewed edge-on) that are mirrored, a distinctive figure. These are easily confused with circulation strikes except for the features noted. Certified holders usually list these simply as "Proof," not "Matte Proof." Some early Proofs of 1936 have satiny rather than mirror-like fields. Later Proofs of 1936 and all of 1937 have a mirror surface in the fields. The motifs of the 1936 and 1937 mirror Proofs are lightly polished in the die (not frosty or matte).

GRADING STANDARDS

MS-60 to 70 (Mint State). *Obverse and Reverse:* Mint luster is complete in the obverse and reverse fields, except in areas not fully struck up, in which graininess or marks from the original planchet surface can be seen. Lower grades such as MS-60, 61, and 62 can show some evidence of abrasion, usually on the center of the

1937-D, 3-Legged. Graded MS-65.

obverse above the braid, and on the reverse at the highest parts of the bison. These two checkpoints are often areas of light striking, so abrasion must be differentiated from original planchet marks. At MS-63 evidences of abrasion are few, and at MS-65 they are fewer yet. In grades above MS-65, a Buffalo nickel should be mark-free.

Illustrated coin: A gem example with exceptional eye appeal, this coin has smooth, satiny surfaces free of toning or notable detractions. An uncommonly sharp strike is also notable, especially on the reverse.

AU-50, 53, 55, 58 (About Uncirculated). *Obverse:* Light wear is seen on the highest area of the cheek, to the left of the nose, this being the most obvious checkpoint. Light wear is also seen on the highest-relief areas of the hair. Luster is less exten- sive, and wear more extensive, at AU-50 than at higher grades. An AU-58 coin will

1918-D, 8 Over 7. Graded AU-58.

have only slight wear and will retain the majority of luster. *Reverse:* Light wear is seen on the shoulder and hip, these being the key checkpoints. Light wear is also seen on the flank of the bison and on the horn and top of the head. Luster is less extensive, and wear more extensive, at AU-50 than at higher grades. An AU-58 coin will have only slight wear and will retain the majority of luster.

Illustrated coin: This lovely example has sharply defined details, though it is slightly light at the centers. This is an exceptional grade for this very rare overdate variety.

EF-40, 45 (Extremely Fine). *Obverse:* More wear is seen on the cheek (in particular) and the rest of the face. The center of the coin above the braid is mostly smooth. Other details are sharp. *Reverse:* More wear is evident. The tip of the horn is well defined on better strikes. The shoulder,

1937-D. Graded EF-40.

flank, and hip show more wear. The tip of the tail may be discernible, but is mostly worn away.

VF-20, 30 (Very Fine). *Obverse:* The hair above the braid is mostly flat, but with some details visible. The braid is discernible. The feathers lack most details. On Variety 1 coins the date is light. *Reverse:* Wear is more extensive, with most fur detail on the high area of the shoulder

1937-D. Graded VF-20.

gone, the tip of the tail gone, and the horn flat. Ideally the tip of the horn should show, but in the marketplace many certified coins do not show this. On some coins this is due to a shallow strike.

F-12, 15 (Fine). *Obverse:* Only slight detail remains in the hair above the braid. Some of the braid twists are blended together. LIBERTY is weak, and on some coins the upper part of the letters is faint. The rim still is separate. On all coins, the date shows extensive wear. On Variety 1 coins it is weak. *Reverse:* The horn is half to two-

1918-D, 8 Over 7.
Graded F-12.

thirds visible. Fur details are gone except on the neck at the highest part of the back.

VG-8, 10 (Very Good). *Obverse:* Hair details above the braid are further worn, as is the hair at the top of the head. Most braid twists are blended together. The rim is worn down to the tops of the letters in LIBERTY. The date is light on all coins and very weak on those of Variety 1. *Reverse:* The base of the horn is slightly vis-

1918-D, 8 Over 7.
Graded VG-8.

ible. Fur details are worn more, but details can still be seen on the neck and top of the back. The hip and flank beneath are worn flat.

G-4, 6 (Good). *Obverse:* Scarcely any hair details are seen at the center, and the braid is flat. The rim and tops of the letters in LIBERTY are blended. The date is weak but readable, with at least the last two numerals showing on earlier issues.

1918-D, 8 Over 7. Graded G-4.

Reverse: The rim is worn to blend into the tops of some or all letters in UNITED STATES OF AMERICA (except for Variety 1). E PLURIBUS UNUM and FIVE CENTS are full, and the mintmark, if any, is clear. The front part of the bison's head blends into the rim.

AG-3 (About Good). *Obverse:* The head is mostly flat, but the facial features remain clear. LIBERTY is weak and partly missing. The date may be incomplete but must be identifiable. *Reverse:* Further wear is seen. On Variety 1 coins, UNITED STATES OF AMERICA is full and readable. On the Variety 2 the rim is worn further into the

1913-S, Variety 2. Graded AG-3.

letters. The reverse of the Variety 1 nickels is bolder as the overall grade is defined by the date, which wore away more quickly than on the Variety 2.

Illustrated coin: This coin is barely identifiable as to date but with its mintmark clear.

PF-60 to 70 (Matte Proof). *Obverse and Reverse:* Most Matte Proofs are in higher grades. Those with abrasion or contact marks can be graded PF-60 to 62; these are not widely desired. PF-64 can have some abrasion. Tiny flecks are not common, but are sometimes seen. At the

1914. Graded Matte PF-67.

Matte PF-65 level or higher there will no traces of abrasion or flecks. Differences between higher-grade Proofs are highly subjective, and one certified at PF-65 can be similar to another at PF-67, and vice-versa.

PF-60 to 70 (Mirror Proof). *Obverse and Reverse:* Most mirror Proofs are in higher grades. PF-60 to 62 coins can have abrasion or minor handling marks, but are usually assigned such grades because of staining or blotches resulting from poor cleaning. PF-63 and 64 can have minor

1916. Graded Mirror PF-67.

abrasion and staining. Tiny flecks are not common, but are sometimes seen, as are dark stripe lines from the glued seams in the cellophane envelopes used by the Mint. PF-65 and higher coins should be free of stains, flecks, and abrasion of any kind. Differences between higher-grade Proofs are highly subjective, and one certified PF-65 can be similar to another at PF-67, and vice-versa.

Illustrated coin: This fully struck Matte Proof example has a satiny sheen and no detracting blemishes. The obverse has a delicate, champagne-gold toning, while the reverse is an attractive silver-blue with pale rose highlights.

WINGED LIBERTY HEAD OR "MERCURY" DIMES (1916–1945)

History. In 1916 a new dime, designed by sculptor Adolph A. Weinman (who also created the half dollar that debuted that year), replaced Charles Barber's Liberty Head type. Officially Weinman's design was known as the Winged Liberty Head, but numismatists commonly call the coin the Mercury dime, from Miss Liberty's wing-capped resemblance to the Roman god. The reverse depicts a fasces (symbolic of strength in unity) and an olive branch (symbolic of peaceful intentions). Production was continuous from 1916 to 1945, except for 1922, 1932, and 1933.

Striking and Sharpness. Many Mercury dimes exhibit areas of light striking, most notably in the center horizontal band across the fasces, less so in the lower horizontal band. The bands are composed of two parallel lines with a separation or "split" between. The term Full Bands, abbreviated FB, describes coins with both parallel lines in the center band distinctly separated. In addition, some dimes may display weak striking in other areas (not noted by certification services or others), including at areas of Liberty's hair, the rim, and the date. Dimes of 1921 in particular can have FB but poorly struck dates. Proof dies were completely polished, including the portrait.

Availability. Certain coins, such as 1916-D; 1921-P; 1921-D; 1942, 2 Over 1; and 1942-D, 2 Over 1, are elusive in any grade. Others are generally available in lower circulated grades, although some are scarce. In MS many of the issues before 1931 range from scarce to rare. If with FB and also sharply struck in other areas, some are rare. MS coins usually are very lustrous. In the marketplace certain scarce early issues such as 1916-D, 1921, and 1921-D are often graded slightly more liberally than are later varieties. Proofs were minted from 1936 to 1942 and are available in proportion to their mintages.

GRADING STANDARDS

MS-60 to 70 (Mint State). *Obverse:* At MS-60, some abrasion and contact marks are evident on the highest part of the portrait, including the hair immediately to the right of the face and the upper left part of the wing. At MS-63, abrasion is slight at best, less so for 64. Album slide

1919-S. Graded MS-65.

marks on the cheek, if present, should not be at any grade above MS-64. An MS-65 coin should display no abrasion or contact marks except under magnification, and MS-66 and higher coins should have none at all. Luster should be full and rich. *Reverse:* Comments apply as for the obverse, except that the highest parts of the fasces, these being the horizontal bands, are the places to check. The field is mainly protected by design elements and does not show contact marks readily.

Illustrated coin: This lustrous example is lightly toned.

AU-50, 53, 55, 58 (About Uncirculated). *Obverse:* Light wear is seen on the cheek, the hair immediately to the right of the face, the left edge of the wing, and the upper right of the wing. At AU-58, the luster is extensive, but incomplete, especially on the higher parts and in the field. At AU-50 and 53, luster is less. *Reverse:* Light

1942, 2 Over 1.
Graded AU-55.

wear is seen on the higher parts of the fasces. An AU-58 coin has nearly full luster, more so than on the obverse, as the design elements protect the field areas. At AU-50 and 53, there still is significant luster. Generally, the reverse appears to be in a slightly higher grade than the obverse.

EF-40, 45 (Extremely Fine). *Obverse:* Further wear is seen on the head. Many of the hair details are blended together, as are some feather details at the left side of the wing. *Reverse:* The horizontal bands on the fasces may be fused together. The diagonal bands remain in slight relief against the vertical lines (sticks).

1921. Graded EF-40.

VF-20, 30 (Very Fine). *Obverse:* The head shows more wear, now with the forehead and cheek mostly blending into the hair. More feather details are gone. *Reverse:* Wear is more extensive, but the diagonal and horizontal bands on the fasces still are separated from the thin vertical sticks.

1942, 2 Over 1. Graded VF-20.

F-12, 15 (Fine). *Obverse:* The head shows more wear, the hair has only slight detail, and most of the feathers are gone. In the marketplace a coin in F-12 grade usually has slightly less detail than stated by the ANA grading standards or Photograde, from modern interpretations. *Reverse:*

1916-D. Graded F-12.

Many of the tiny vertical sticks in the fasces are blended together. The bands can be barely discerned and may be worn away at the highest-relief parts.

VG-8, 10 (Very Good). *Obverse:* Wear is more extensive on the portrait, and only a few feathers are seen on the wing. The outlines between the hair and cap and of the wing are distinct. Lettering is clear, but light in areas. *Reverse:* The rim is complete, or it may be slightly worn away in

1916-D. Graded VG-8.

areas. Only a few traces of the vertical sticks remain in the fasces. Current interpretations in the marketplace are given here and are less strict than those listed by the ANA grading standards and *Photograde.* Often, earlier issues are graded more liberally than are later dates.

G-4, 6 (Good). *Obverse:* Wear is more extensive, with not all of the outline between the hair and the wing visible. The rim is worn into the edges of the letters and often into the bottom of the last numeral in the date. *Reverse:* The rim is worn away, as are the outer parts of the letters.

1916-D. Graded G-4.

The fasces is flat or may show a hint of a vertical stick or two. The leaves are thick from wear. The mintmark, if any, is easily seen.

AG-3 (About Good). *Obverse:* The rim is worn further into the letters. The head is mostly outline all over, except for a few indicates of edges. Folds remain at the top of the cap. The date is clearly visible. *Reverse:* The rim is worn further into the letters. The mintmark, if any, is clear but

1916-D. Graded AG-3.

may be worn away slightly at the bottom. The apparent wear is slightly greater on the reverse than on the obverse.

PF-60 to 70 (Proof). *Obverse and Reverse:* Proofs that are extensively cleaned and have many hairlines, or that are dull and grainy, are lower level, such as PF-60 to 62. These are not widely desired, and represent coins that have been mistreated. With medium hairlines and good reflec-

1939. Graded PF-67.

tivity, assigned grades of PF-63 or 64 are appropriate. Tiny horizontal lines on Miss Liberty's cheek, known as slide marks, from National and other album slides scuffing the relief of the cheek, are common; coins with such marks should not be graded higher than PF-64, but sometimes are. With relatively few hairlines and no noticeable slide marks, a rating of PF-65 can be given. PF-66 should have hairlines so delicate that magnification is needed to see them. Above that, a Proof should be free of any hairlines or other problems.

STANDING LIBERTY QUARTERS (1916–1930)

History. The Standing Liberty quarter dollar, designed by sculptor Hermon A. MacNeil (whose initial, M, is located above and to the right of the date), was greeted with wide acclaimed from its first appearance. All of

1916 and many of 1917 are of the Variety 1 design, with the right breast of Miss Liberty exposed on the obverse and with no stars below the eagle on the reverse. Variety 2 of the Standing Liberty design was introduced in 1917 and continued to the end of the series. Miss Liberty is clothed in a jacket of chainmail armor, and the reverse is slightly redesigned, with stars below the eagle. These changes came at the suggestion of the designer, Hermon A. MacNeil.

Striking and Sharpness. Many if not most 1916 quarters are somewhat lightly struck on the head and body of Miss Liberty. The 1917, Variety 1, quarters usually are quite well struck. When light striking is found, it is usually on the higher-relief parts of the head, the right knee (not as obvious), and the rivets on the left side of the shield. The 1917 Philadelphia Mint coins are usually sharper than the other varieties of this type. Most coins of the Variety 2 design have areas of light striking. On the obverse these are most notable on the head of Miss Liberty and on the shield, the latter often with the two lower-left rivets weak or missing and with the center emblem on the shield weak. The center of the standing figure can be weak as well, as can the upper-left area at and near the date. After 1924 the date was slightly recessed, eliminating that problem. On the reverse, check the eagle's breast. A misleading term, Full Head (FH), is widely used to describe quarters that have only partial head details; such coins often actually have the two lower-left shield rivets poorly struck or not visible at all. Most third-party grading services define these criteria for "Full Head" designation (in order of importance): a full, unbroken hairline from Liberty's brow down to the jawline; all three leaves on the head showing; and a visible ear hole.

Availability. The 1916 quarter is the key to the series. Examples tend to be liberally graded in the reallife marketplace, especially in EF and AU, this in contrast to more careful grading for the less valuable 1917 issues. Circulated coins of 1916 and 1917 often have the date worn partly away, due to the high position of this feature in the design. Among Variety 2 coins, the 1918-S, 8 Over 7, is recognized as the key issue, and the 1919-D, 1921, 1923-S, and 1927-S as quite scarce. MS coins are readily available for most issues, but Full Details coins can be extreme rarities. Circulated coins dated from 1917 through 1924 often have the date worn partly away, due to the high position of this feature in the design. On MS coins the luster usually is rich and attractive. No Proof coins of this type were officially issued, but specimen strikings dated 1917 are known to exist.

GRADING STANDARDS

MS-60 to 70 (Mint State). *Obverse:* At MS-60 some abrasion and contact marks are evident on the higher areas, which are also the areas most likely to be weakly struck. This includes the rivets on the shield to the left and the central escutcheon on the shield,

1917, No Stars. Graded MS-67.

the head, and the right leg of Miss Liberty. The luster may not be complete in those areas on weakly struck coins, even those certified above MS-65—the original planchet surface may be revealed as it was not smoothed out by striking. Accordingly, grading is best done by evaluating abrasion and mint luster as it is observed. Luster may be dull or lifeless at MS-60 to 62 but should have deep frost at MS-63 or better, particularly in the lower-relief areas. At MS-65 or better, it should be full and rich. *Reverse:* Striking is usually quite good, permitting observation of luster in all areas. Check the eagle's breast and the surface of the right wing. Luster may be dull or lifeless at MS-60 to 62 but should have deep frost at MS-63 or better, particularly in the lower-relief areas. At MS-65 or better, it should be full and rich.

Illustrated coin: This gorgeous coin has sharply struck details and full luster.

AU-50, 53, 55, 58 (About Uncirculated). *Obverse:* Light wear is seen on the figure of Miss Liberty, especially noticeable around her midriff and right knee. The shield shows wear, as does the highest part of the sash where it crosses Miss Liberty's waist. At

1916. Graded AU-55.

AU-58 the luster is extensive, but incomplete on the higher areas, although it should be nearly full in the panels of the parapet to the left and right, and in the upper field. At AU-50 and 53, luster is less. *Reverse:* Wear is most evident on the eagle's breast, the edges of both wings, and the interior area of the right wing. Luster is nearly complete at AU-58, but at AU-50, half or more is gone.

Illustrated coin: The original luster is still present in some areas of this lightly struck coin.

EF-40, 45 (Extremely Fine). *Obverse:* Wear is more extensive, with the higher parts of Miss Liberty now without detail and the front of the right leg flat. The shield is worn. On coins dated from 1917 to 1924 the date shows wear at the top (on those of 1925

1927-S. Graded EF-40.

to 1930, with the date recessed, the numbers are bold). Little or no luster is seen, except perhaps among the letters. *Reverse:* The eagle shows more wear, with the surface of the right wing being mostly flat. Little or no luster is evident.

VF-20, 30 (Very Fine). *Obverse:* Wear is more extensive. The higher-relief areas of Miss Liberty are flat, and the sash crossing her waist is mostly blended into it (some sharply struck pieces being exceptions). The left side of the shield is mostly

1927-S. Graded VF-20.

flat, although its outline can be seen. On quarters dated 1917 to 1924 the top of the date shows more wear. *Reverse:* The eagle shows further wear, with the body blending into the wing above it. Much feather detail is gone from the wing to the left (on quarters dated 1925 to 1930; less so for those dated 1917 to 1924). Most detail is gone from the right wing.

F-12, 15 (Fine). *Obverse:* Miss Liberty is worn nearly flat. Most detail in her gown is gone, except to the left of her leg and below her knee to the right. The stars on the parapet are well worn, with some indistinct. The top of the date is weak. Quarters of the

1916. Graded F-12.

rare 1916 date are slightly weaker than those of 1917 in this and lower grades. On quarters of 1917 to 1924 the top of the date is weak. On those dated 1925 to 1930 the date remains strong. *Reverse:* The eagle shows further wear, this being greater on 1925 to 1930 issues than on the earlier dates.

VG-8, 10 (Very Good). *Obverse:* The obverse is worn further, with fewer details in the skirt, and part of the shield border to the left blended into the standing figure. The date is partially worn away at the top, and quarters from 1917 to 1924 have less

1917, No Stars. Graded VG-8.

detail. Those from 1925 to 1930 retain more detail, and the date is full. *Reverse:* The eagle is worn further, with only about a third of the feathers now discernible, these mostly on the wing to the left.

G-4, 6 (Good). *Obverse:* The wear is more extensive. Most coins have the stars missing, the standing figure flat, and much of the date worn away, although still clearly identifiable. Quarters of 1925 to 1930 show more detail and the date is clear. *Reverse:* The

1927. Graded G-6.

eagle is mostly in outline form, with only a few feather details visible. The rim is worn into the letters, and on quarters of 1916 to 1924, E PLURIBUS UNUM is very faint; it is clear on quarters of later dates.

AG-3 (About Good). *Obverse:* The obverse is worn nearly smooth, and the date is mostly gone. On some coins just one or two digits are seen. Fortunately, those digits are usually on the right, such as a trace of just a 6, which will identify the coin as a

1927. Graded AG-3.

1916. On quarters of 1925 to 1930 the wear is more extensive than for G-4, but most features are discernible and the date is clear. *Reverse:* The eagle is flat, and the border is worn down further. On quarters of 1916 to 1924, E PLURIBUS UNUM is extremely faint or even missing in areas; it remains readable on quarters of later dates.

WASHINGTON, EAGLE REVERSE, QUARTERS (1932–1998)

History. The Washington quarter, designed by New York sculptor John Flanagan, originally was intended to be a commemorative coin, but it ultimately was produced as a regular circulation issue. The obverse is inspired by a famous bust by Jean Antoine Houdon. Flanagan's initials, JF, are at the base of Washington's neck. The reverse features a modernistic eagle perched on a quiver of arrows, with wings unfolding. In October 1973, the Treasury Department announced an open contest for the selection of suitable designs for the Bicentennial reverses of the quarter, half dollar, and dollar, with $5,000 to be awarded to each winner. Twelve semifinalists were chosen, and from these the symbolic entry of Jack L. Ahr was selected for the quarter reverse. It features a military drummer facing left, with a victory torch encircled by 13 stars at the upper left. Except for the dual dating, "1776–1976," the obverse remained unchanged. Pieces with this dual dating were coined during 1975 and 1976. They were struck for general circulation and included in all the U.S. Mint's offerings of Proof and Uncirculated coin sets. (The grading instructions below are for the regular Eagle Reverse variety.)

Striking and Sharpness. The relief of both sides of the Washington quarter issues from 1932 to 1998 is shallow. Accordingly, any lightness of strike is not easily seen. Nearly all are well struck. On all quarters of 1932 and some of 1934, the motto IN GOD WE TRUST is light, as per the design. It was strengthened in 1934.

Availability. The 1932-D and S are key issues but not rarities. All others are readily available in high grades, but some are scarcer than others. Proof dates available are 1936 to 1942 and 1950 to 1964 (from the Philadelphia Mint) and 1968 to 1998 (from San Francisco). Certain later Proofs are available in clad metal as well as silver strikings. Special Mint Set (SMS) coins were struck in lieu of Proofs from 1965 to 1967; these in some instances closely resemble Proofs. The majority of Proofs made in recent decades are in high levels, PF-66 to 68 or higher.

GRADING STANDARDS

MS-60 to 70 (Mint State). *Obverse:* At MS-60, some abrasion and contact marks are evident on the hair above the ear and at the top of the head below E of LIBERTY. At MS-63, abrasion is slight at best, less so for MS-64. An MS-65 coin should display no abrasion

1932-S. Graded MS-64.

or contact marks except under magnification, and MS-66 and higher coins should have none at all. Luster should be full and rich. *Reverse:* Comments apply as for the obverse, except that the eagle's breast and legs are the places to check. On both sides the fields are protected by design elements and do not show contact marks readily.

   Illustrated coin: This is a brilliant and lustrous example with excellent eye appeal.

AU-50, 53, 55, 58 (About Uncirculated). *Obverse:* Light wear is seen on the cheek, the high areas of the hair, and the neck. At AU-58, the luster is extensive but incomplete, especially on the higher parts and in the field. At AU-50 and 53, luster is less.

1932-D. Graded AU-53.

Reverse: Light wear is seen on the breast, legs, and upper edges of the wings of the eagle. An AU-58 coin has nearly full luster. At AU-50 and 53, there still is significant luster.

   Illustrated coin: Some of the original luster remains on the obverse of this example, while most of the luster remains on the reverse.

EF-40, 45 (Extremely Fine). *Obverse:* Further wear is seen on the head. Higher-relief details are gone in the hair. The higher-relief parts of the neck show wear, most noticeably just above the date. *Reverse:* Further wear is seen on the eagle. Most breast

1940. Graded EF-40.

feathers, not strong to begin with, are worn away.

VF-20, 30 (Very Fine). *Obverse:* Most hair detail is worn away, except above the curls. The delineation between the temple and the edge of the hair is faint. The curl by the ear is worn flat. Tips of the letters in LIBERTY and the date digits touch the rim

1937. Graded VF-20.

in some instances. *Reverse:* More details of the eagle are worn away, and the outlines of the feathers in the wing, while nearly all present, are faint. Tips of the letters touch the rim in some instances on this and lower grades, but this can vary from coin to coin depending on the strength of the rim.

F-12, 15 (Fine). *Obverse:* Most of the hair is worn flat, with no distinction between the face and the beginning of the hair. There is some detail remaining just above and below the curls. *Reverse:* More feathers are worn away. The end of the branch at the left is worn so as to blend

1934, Doubled-Die Obverse. Graded F-12.

into the wing. The edge of the rim is barely visible and in some areas is worn away. (In this and the Very Good grade, opinions concerning the rim vary in the ANA grading standards and in *Photograde*, PCGS is silent on the matter.)

VG-8, 10 (Very Good). *Obverse:* Further wear is seen on the head, with most of the upper part of the curls now blending into the hair above. *Reverse:* The rim is worn into the tops of the letters. There is no detail on the leaves. About half of the feathers are outlined, but only faintly.

1935-D. Graded VG-8.

G-4, 6 (Good). *Obverse:* Further wear is seen in all areas. On 1932 and some 1934 coins the IN GOD WE TRUST motto is so worn that some letters are missing. *Reverse:* The rim is worn further into the letters. Fewer details are seen on the eagle's wing. On

1932-D. Graded G-4.

both sides the coin appears to be "worn flat," with little in relief.

AG-3 (About Good). *Obverse:* Wear is more extensive, with about half of the letters gone. *Reverse:* Wear is more extensive, with about half of the letters gone. Slight detail remains in the eagle's wings. The mintmark, if any, is very clear.

1942. Graded AG-3.

PF-60 to 70 (Proof). *Obverse and Reverse:* Proofs that are extensively cleaned and have many hairlines, or that are dull and grainy, are lower level, such as PF-60 to 62. These are not widely desired, and represent coins that have been mistreated. Most low-

1938. Graded PF-66.

level Proofs are of the 1936 to 1942 dates. With medium hairlines and good reflectivity, assigned grades of PF-63 or 64 are appropriate. PF-66 should have hairlines so delicate that magnification is needed to see them. Above that, a Proof should be free of any hairlines or other problems.

BARBER OR LIBERTY HEAD HALF DOLLARS (1892–1915)

History. Charles E. Barber, chief engraver of the U.S. Mint, crafted the eponymous "Barber" or Liberty Head half dollars along with similarly designed dimes and quarters of the same era. His initial, B, is at the truncation of Miss Liberty's neck. Production of the coins was continuous from 1892 to 1915, stopping a year before the dime and quarter of the same design.

Striking and Sharpness. On the obverse, check Miss Liberty's hair details and other features. On the reverse, the eagle's leg at the lower right and the arrows often are weak, and there can be weakness at the upper right of the shield and the nearby wing area. At EF and below, sharpness of strike on the reverse is not important. Most Proofs are sharply struck, although many are weak on the eagle's leg at the lower right and on certain parts of the arrows and/or the upper-right area of the shield and the nearby wing. The Proofs of 1892 to 1901 usually have cameo contrast between the designs and the mirror fields. Those of 1914 and 1915 are often with extensive hairlines or other problems.

Availability. Most examples seen in the marketplace are well worn. There are no rarities in the Barber half dollar series, although some are scarcer than others. Coins that are Fine or better are much scarcer—in particular the San Francisco Mint issues of 1901, 1904, and 1907. MS coins are available of all dates and mints, but some are very elusive. Proofs exist in proportion to their mintages. Choicer examples tend to be of later dates, similar to other Barber coins.

GRADING STANDARDS

MS-60 to 70 (Mint State). *Obverse:* At MS-60, some abrasion and contact marks are evident, most noticeably on the cheek and the obverse field to the right. Luster is present, but may be dull or lifeless. Many Barber coins have been cleaned, especially of the

1909. Graded MS-62.

earlier dates. At MS-63, contact marks are very few; abrasion still is evident but less than at lower levels. Indeed, the cheek of Miss Liberty virtually showcases abrasion. This is even more evident on a half dollar than on lower denominations. An MS-65 coin may have minor abrasion, but contact marks are so minute as to require magnification. Luster should be full and rich. *Reverse:* Comments apply as for the obverse, except that in lower Mint State grades abrasion and contact marks are most noticeable on the head and tail of the eagle and on the tips of the wings. At MS-65 or higher there are no marks visible to the unaided eye. The field is mainly protected by design elements, so the reverse often appears to grade a point or two higher than the obverse.

Illustrated coin: On this example, mottled light-brown toning appears over lustrous surfaces.

AU-50, 53, 55, 58 (About Uncirculated). *Obverse:* Light wear is seen on the head, especially on the forward hair under LIBERTY. At AU-58, the luster is extensive but incomplete, especially on the higher parts and in the right field. At AU-50 and 53, luster is

1915-D. Graded AU-53.

less. *Reverse:* Wear is seen on the head and tail of the eagle and on the tips of the wings. At AU-50 and 53, there still is significant luster. An AU-58 coin (as determined by the obverse) can have the reverse appear to be full Mint State.

Illustrated coin: Areas of original Mint luster can be seen on this coin, more so on the reverse than on the obverse.

EF-40, 45 (Extremely Fine). *Obverse:* Further wear is seen on the head. The hair above the forehead lacks most detail. LIBERTY shows wear but still is strong. *Reverse:* Further wear is seen on the head and tail of the eagle and on the tips of the

1908-S. Graded EF-45.

wings, most evident at the left and right extremes of the wings At this level and below, sharpness of strike on the reverse is not important.

VF-20, 30 (Very Fine). *Obverse:* The head shows more wear, now with nearly all detail gone in the hair above the forehead. LIBERTY shows wear, but is complete. The leaves on the head all show wear, as does the upper part of the cap. *Reverse:* Wear is

1897-S. Graded VF-30.

more extensive, particularly noticeable on the outer parts of the wings, the head, the shield, and the tail.

    Illustrated coin: This coin is seemingly lightly cleaned.

F-12, 15 (Fine). *Obverse:* The head shows extensive wear. LIBERTY, the key place to check, is weak, especially at ER, but is fully readable. The ANA grading standards and *Photograde* adhere to this. PCGS suggests that lightly struck coins "may have letters

1909-O. Graded F-12.

partially missing." Traditionally, collectors insist on full LIBERTY. *Reverse:* More wear is seen on the reverse, in the places as above. E PLURIBUS UNUM is light, with one to several letters worn away.

VG-8, 10 (Very Good). *Obverse:* A net of three letters in LIBERTY must be readable. Traditionally LI is clear, and after that there is a partial letter or two. *Reverse:* Further wear has smoothed more than half of the feathers in the wing. The shield is indistinct

1915-S. Graded VG-8.

except for a few traces of interior lines. The motto is partially worn away. The rim is full, and many if not most denticles can be seen.

G-4, 6 (Good). *Obverse:* The head is in outline form, with the center flat. Most of the rim is there and all letters and the date are full. *Reverse:* The eagle shows only a few feathers, and only a few scattered letters remain in the motto. The rim may be worn flat in some or all of the area, but the peripheral lettering is clear.

1892-O. Graded G-4.

Illustrated coin: On this coin the obverse is perhaps G-6 and the reverse AG-3. The grade might be averaged as G-4.

AG-3 (About Good). *Obverse:* The stars and motto are worn, and the border may be indistinct. Distinctness varies at this level. The date is clear. Grading is usually determined by the reverse. *Reverse:* The rim is gone and the letters are partially worn

1896-S. Graded AG-3.

away. The eagle is mostly flat, perhaps with a few hints of feathers. Usually, the obverse appears to be in a slightly higher grade than the reverse.

PF-60 to 70 (Proof). *Obverse and Reverse:* Proofs that are extensively cleaned and have many hairlines, or that are dull and grainy, are lower level, such as PF-60 to 62; these are not widely desired. With medium hairlines and good reflectivity, an assigned

1914. Graded PF-61.

grade of PF-64 is appropriate. Tiny horizontal lines on Miss Liberty's cheek, known as slide marks, from National and other album slides scuffing the relief of the cheek, are endemic on all Barber silver coins. With noticeable marks of this type, the highest grade assignable is PF-64. With relatively few hairlines, a rating of PF-65 can be given. PF-66 should have hairlines so delicate that magnification is needed to see them. Above that, a Proof should be free of any hairlines or other problems.

Illustrated coin: This is an attractive coin at the relatively low PF-61 grade.

LIBERTY WALKING HALF DOLLARS (1916–1947)

History. The Liberty Walking half dollar was designed by Adolph A. Weinman, the sculptor who also created the Mercury or Winged Liberty Head dime. His monogram appears under the tips of the eagle's wing feathers. Mintage was intermittent from 1916 to 1947, with none struck in 1922, 1924, 1925, 1926, 1930, 1931, and 1932. On the 1916 coins and some of the 1917 coins, the mintmark is located on the obverse, below IN GOD WE TRUST. Other coins of 1917, and those through 1947, have the mintmark on the reverse, under the pine branch.

Striking and Sharpness. Most circulation-strike Liberty Walking half dollars are lightly struck. In this respect they are similar to Standing Liberty quarters of the same era. On the obverse, the key points to check are Miss Liberty's left hand, the higher parts and lines in the skirt, and her head; after that, check all other areas. Very few coins are sharply struck in these areas, and for some issues sharp strikes might not exist at all. On the reverse, check the breast of the eagle. Proofs were made beginning in 1936 and continuing through 1942. The entire die was polished (including the figure of Miss Liberty and the eagle), generating coins of low contrast. Proofs are usually fairly well struck. Most Proofs of 1941 are from over-polished dies, with the AW monogram of the designer no longer present. Striking sharpness can vary. Seek coins with full head and left-hand details.

Availability. All dates and mintmarks are readily collectible, although some, such as 1917-S (obverse mintmark), 1919-D, the three issues of 1921, and 1938-D, are scarce. Earlier years are often seen with extensive wear. MS coins are most often seen of the three issues of 1916, the 1917, and those of 1933 to 1947. Collectors saved the issues of the 1940s in large quantities, making the coins common today. As noted, coins with Full Details can range from scarce to extremely rare for certain dates. Half dollars dated 1928-D are counterfeit.

GRADING STANDARDS

MS-60 to 70 (Mint State). *Obverse:* At MS-60, some abrasion and contact marks are evident on the higher areas, which are also the areas most likely to be weakly struck. This includes Miss Liberty's left arm, her hand, and the areas of the skirt covering her

1917. Graded MS-65.

left leg. The luster may not be complete in those areas on weakly struck coins (even those certified above MS-65)—the original planchet surface may be revealed, as it was not smoothed out by striking. Accordingly, grading is best done by evaluating abrasion as it is observed in the right field, plus evaluating the mint luster. Luster may be dull or lifeless at MS-60 to 62, but should have deep frost at MS-63 or better, particularly in the lower-relief areas. At MS-65 or better, it should be full and rich. Sometimes, to compensate for flat striking, certified coins with virtually flawless luster in the fields, evocative of an MS-65 or 66 grade, are called MS-63 or a lower grade. Such coins would seem to offer a lot of value for the money, if the variety is one that is not found with Full Details (1923-S is one of many examples). *Reverse:* Striking is usually better, permitting observation of luster in all areas except the eagle's body, which may be lightly struck. Luster may be dull or lifeless at MS-60 to 62, but should have deep frost at MS-63 or better, particularly in the lower-relief areas. At MS-65 or better, it should be full and rich.

Illustrated coin: This is a lustrous gem example.

AU-50, 53, 55, 58 (About Uncirculated). *Obverse:* Light wear is seen on the higher-relief areas of Miss Liberty, the vertical area from her head down to the date. At AU-58, the luster in the field is extensive, but is interrupted by friction and light wear. At AU-50

1921-S. Graded AU-50.

and 53, luster is less. *Reverse:* Wear is most evident on the eagle's breast immediately under the neck feathers, the left leg, and the top of the left wing. Luster is nearly complete at AU-58, but at AU-50 half or more is gone.

EF-40, 45 (Extremely Fine). *Obverse:* Wear is more extensive, with the higher parts of Miss Liberty now without detail, and with no skirt lines visible directly over her left leg. Little or no luster is seen. *Reverse:* The eagle shows

1919-S. Graded EF-40.

more wear overall, with the highest parts of the body and left leg worn flat.

VF-20, 30 (Very Fine). *Obverse:* Wear is more extensive, and Miss Liberty is worn mostly flat in the line from her head to her left foot. Her skirt is worn, but most lines are seen, except over the leg and to the left and right. The lower part of her cape (to the left

1921-S. Graded VF-20.

of her waist) is worn. *Reverse:* The eagle is worn smooth from the head to the left leg, and the right leg is flat at the top. Most feathers in the wings are delineated, but weak.

F-12, 15 (Fine). *Obverse:* Wear is more extensive, now with only a few light lines visible in the skirt. The rays of the sun are weak below the cape, and may be worn away at their tips. *Reverse:* Wear is more extensive, with most details now gone on the eagle's right

1918-S. Graded F-12.

leg. Delineation of the feathers is less, and most in the upper area and right edge of the left wing are blended together.

VG-8, 10 (Very Good). *Obverse:* Wear is slightly more extensive, but the rim still is defined all around. The tops of the date numerals are worn and blend slightly into the ground above. *Reverse:* Wear is more extensive. On the left wing only a few feath-

1921-D. Graded VG-8.

ers are delineated, and on the shoulder of the right wing most detail is gone. Detail in the pine branch is lost and it appears as a clump.

G-4, 6 (Good). *Obverse:* Miss Liberty is worn flat, with her head, neck, and arms all blended together. Folds can be seen at the bottom of the skirt, but the lines are worn away. The rim is worn done into the tops of some of the letters. *Reverse:* All areas show more wear. The rim is worn

1917-S, Obverse Mintmark.
Graded G-4.

down into the tops of some of the letters, particularly at the top border.

AG-3 (About Good). *Obverse:* Wear is more extensive. The sun's rays are nearly all gone, the motto is very light and sometimes incomplete, and the rim is worn down into more of the letters. *Reverse:* Wear is more extensive, with the eagle essentially

1918. Graded AG-3.

worn flat. The rim is worn down into more of the letters.

PF-60 to 70 (Proof). *Obverse and Reverse:* Proofs that are extensively cleaned and have many hairlines, or that are dull and grainy, are lower level, such as PF-60 to 62. These are not widely desired, and represent coins that have been mistreated. With

1939. Graded PF-65.

medium hairlines and good reflectivity, assigned grades of PF-63 or 64 are appropriate. Tiny horizontal lines on Miss Liberty's leg, known as slide marks, from National and other album slides scuffing the relief of the cheek, are common; coins with such marks should not be graded higher than PF-64, but sometimes are. With relatively few hairlines and no noticeable slide marks, a rating of PF-65 can be given. PF-66 should have hairlines so delicate that magnification is needed to see them. Above that, a Proof should be free of any hairlines or other problems.

Illustrated coin: This example is a brilliant gem Proof.

MORGAN DOLLARS (1878-1921)

History. The Morgan dollar, named for English-born designer George T. Morgan, was struck every year from 1878 to 1904, and again in 1921. The coin's production benefited Western silver interests by creating an artificial federal demand for the metal, whose market value had dropped sharply by 1878. Hundreds of millions of the coins, stored in cloth bags of 1,000 each, piled up in government vaults. In the 1900s some were melted, but immense quantities were bought by collectors and investors; today they are the most widely collected of all coins of their era.

Striking and Sharpness. On coins of 1878 to 1900, check the hair above Miss Liberty's ear and, on the reverse, the breast feathers of the eagle. These are weak on many issues, particularly those of the New Orleans Mint. From 1900 to 1904 a new reverse hub was used, and breast feathers, while discernible, are not as sharp. In 1921 new dies were made in lower relief, with certain areas indistinct. Many Morgan dollars have partially or fully prooflike surfaces. These are designated as Prooflike (PL), Deep Prooflike (DPL), or Deep Mirror Prooflike (DMPL). Certification practices can be erratic, and some DMPL-certified coins are not fully mirrored. All prooflike coins tend to emphasize contact marks, with the result that lower MS levels can be unattractive. *A Guide Book of Morgan Silver Dollars* (Bowers) and other references furnish information as to which dates and mintmarks are easily found with Full Details and which usually are weak, as well as the availability of the various levels of prooflike surface.

Proofs were struck from 1878 to 1904, with those of 1878 to 1901 generally having cameo contrast, and 1902 to 1904 having the portrait lightly polished in the die. Some are lightly struck; check the hair above Liberty's ear (in particular), and the eagle's breast feathers. In 1921 many so-called Zerbe Proofs (named thus after numismatic entrepreneur Farran Zerbe), with many microscopic die-finish lines, were made. A very few deeply mirrored 1921 coins were made, called Chapman Proofs (after coin dealer Henry Chapman, who started marketing them shortly after their production). Some Zerbe Proofs have been miscertified as Chapman Proofs.

Availability. All dates and mints of Morgan dollars are available in grades from well worn to MS. Some issues such as certain Carson City coins are rare if worn and common in MS. Other issues such as the 1901 Philadelphia coins are common if worn and are rarities at MS-65. The 1889-CC and 1893-S, and the Proof 1895, are considered to be the key issues. Varieties listed herein are some of those most significant to collectors. Numerous other variations exist, studied in the *Cherrypickers' Guide to Rare Die Varieties* and other specialized texts. Values shown herein are for the most common pieces. Values of varieties not listed in this guide depend on collector interest and demand.

GRADING STANDARDS

MS-60 to 70 (Mint State). *Obverse:* At MS-60, some abrasion and contact marks are evident, most noticeably on the cheek and on the hair above the ear. The left field also shows such marks. Luster is present, but may be dull or lifeless. At MS-63, contact marks

1895-O. Graded MS-61.

are extensive but not distracting. Abrasion still is evident, but less than at lower levels. Indeed, the cheek of Miss Liberty showcases abrasion. An MS-65 coin may have minor abrasion, but contact marks are so minute as to require magnification. Luster should be full and rich. Coins with prooflike surfaces such as PL, DPL, and DMPL display abrasion and contact marks much more noticeably than coins with frosty surfaces; in grades below MS-64 many are unattractive. With today's loose and sometimes contradictory interpretations, many at MS-64 appear to have extensive marks as well. *Reverse:* Comments apply as for the obverse, except that in lower Mint State grades abrasion and contact marks are most noticeable on the eagle's breast. At MS-65 or higher there are no marks visible to the unaided eye. The field is mainly protected by design elements, so the reverse often appears to grade a point or two higher than the obverse. A Morgan dollar can have an MS-63 obverse and an MS-65 reverse, as was indeed the nomenclature used prior to the single-number system. A careful cataloger may want to describe each side separately for a particularly valuable or rare Morgan dollar. An example with an MS-63 obverse and an MS-65 reverse should have an overall grade of MS-63, as the obverse is traditionally given prominence.

Illustrated coin: This is a lustrous and attractive example.

AU-50, 53, 55, 58 (About Uncirculated). *Obverse:* Light wear is seen on the cheek and, to a lesser extent, on the hair below the coronet. Generally, the hair details mask friction and wear and it is not as easy to notice as on the cheek and in the fields. At

1889-CC. Graded AU-58.

AU-58, the luster is extensive, but incomplete, especially on the higher parts and in the left field. At AU-50 and 53, luster is less, but still is present. PL, DPL, and DMPL coins are not widely desired at these levels, as the marks are too distracting. *Reverse:* Wear is evident on the head, breast, wing tips, and, to a lesser extent, in the field. An AU-58 coin (as determined by the obverse) can have a reverse that appears to be full Mint State. (Incidentally, this is also true of Barber quarter dollars and half dollars.)

Illustrated coin: This is a lustrous example of the rarest Carson City Morgan dollar. As is typical of AU-58 dollars of this design, the reverse appears to be full Mint State, as the field is protected by the design elements.

EF-40, 45 (Extremely Fine). *Obverse:* Further wear is seen on the cheek in particular. The hair near the forehead and temple has flatness in areas, most noticeable above the ear. Some luster can be seen in protected areas on many coins, but is not needed

1879-CC. Graded EF-40.

to define the EF-40 and 45 grades. *Reverse:* Further wear is seen on the breast of the eagle (most noticeably), the wing tips, and the leaves.

VF-20, 30 (Very Fine). *Obverse:* The head shows more wear, now with most of the detail gone in the areas adjacent to the forehead and temple. The lower area has most hair fused into large strands. *Reverse:* Wear is more extensive on the breast and on

1889-CC. Graded VF-20.

the feathers in the upper area of the wings, especially the right wing, and on the legs. The high area of the leaves has no detail.

F-12, 15 (Fine). *Obverse:* The head shows more wear, with most hair detail gone, and with a large flat area above the ear. Less detail is seen in the lower curls. *Reverse:* More wear is seen on the reverse, with the eagle's breast and legs flat and about a third of the feather detail gone, mostly near the tops of the wings.

1893-S. Graded F-15.

VG-8, 10 (Very Good). *Obverse:* More hair details are gone, especially from the area from the top of the head down to the ear. The details of the lower part of the cap are gone. The rim is weak in areas, and some denticles are worn away. *Reverse:* Further wear has smoothed more than half of the feathers in the wing. The leaves are flat except for the lowest areas. The rim is weak in areas.

1892-CC. Graded VG-8.

G-4, 6 (Good). *Obverse:* The head is in out- line form, with most details gone. LIBERTY still is readable. The eye position and lips are discernible. Most of the rim is worn away. *Reverse:* The eagle shows some feathers near the bottom of the wings, but nearly all others are gone. The leaves are seen in outline form. The rim is mostly worn away. Some letters have details toward the border worn away.

1893-S. Graded G-4.

The Morgan dollar is seldom collected in grades lower than G-4.

Illustrated coin: Here is a well-worn example of this key issue.

PF-60 to 70 (Proof). *Obverse and Reverse:* Dull, grainy Proofs, or extensively cleaned ones with many hairlines, are lower level (PF-60 to 62). Only the 1895 is desirable at such low grades. Those with medium hairlines and good reflectivity may grade

1898. Graded PF-64.

at about PF-64, and with relatively few hairlines, Gem PF-65. Hairlines are most easily seen in the obverse field. Horizontal slide marks on Miss Liberty's cheek, caused by clear slides on some coin albums, are common. PF-66 may have hairlines so delicate that magnification is needed to see them. Above that, a Proof should be free of such lines, including slide marks.

PEACE DOLLARS (1921–1935)

History. In 1921, following the melting of more than 270 million silver dollars as legislated by the Pittman Act of 1918, the U.S. Treasury struck millions more silver dollars of the Morgan type while a new Peace dollar was in development. Sculptor and medalist Anthony de Francisci created the Peace design, originally intended as a commemorative of the end of the hostilities of the Great War. The obverse features a flowing-haired Miss Liberty wearing a spiked tiara, and the reverse an eagle perched before the rising sun. The designer's monogram is located in the field of the coin under the neck of Miss Liberty. Coins of 1921 were struck in high relief; this caused weakness at the centers, so the design was changed to low relief in 1922. The dollars were struck until 1928, then again in 1934 and 1935. Legislation dated August 3, 1964, authorized the coinage of 45 million silver dollars, and 316,076 dollars of the Peace design dated 1964 were struck at the Denver Mint in 1965. Plans for completing this coinage were subsequently abandoned and all of these coins were melted. None were preserved or released for circulation; details are found in *A Guide Book of Peace Dollars* (Burdette).

Striking and Sharpness. Peace dollars of 1921 are always lightly struck at the center of the obverse, with hair detail not showing in an area. The size of this flat spot can vary. For this and other Peace dollars, check the hair detail at the center and, on the reverse, the feathers on the eagle. Many coins are struck from overly used dies, giving a grainy appearance to the fields, particularly the obverse. On many Peace dollars tiny white "milk spots" are seen, left over from when they were struck; these are not as desirable in the marketplace as unspotted coins.

Availability. All dates and mintmarks are readily available. Although some are well worn, they are generally collected in EF and finer grades. MS coins are available for each, with the 1934-S considered to be the key date. San Francisco issues of the 1920s, except for 1926-S, are often heavily bagmarked from coming into contact with other coins during shipment, storage, and other handling. The appearance of luster varies from issue to issue and can be deeply frosty, or—in the instance of Philadelphia Mint coins of 1928, 1934, and 1935—satiny or "creamy."

Proofs. Some Sandblast Proofs were made in 1921 and a limited issue in 1922 in high relief. These are rare today. Seemingly, a few Satin Proofs were also made in 1921. Sandblast Proofs of 1922 have a peculiar whitish surface in most instances, sometimes interrupted by small dark flecks or spots. There are a number of impostors among certified "Proofs."

Grading Standards

MS-60 to 70 (Mint State). *Obverse:* At MS-60, some abrasion and contact marks are evident, most noticeably on the cheek and on the hair to the right of the face and forehead. Luster is present, but may be dull or lifeless. At MS-63, contact marks are exten-

1921. Graded MS-64.

sive but not distracting. Abrasion still is evident, but less than at lower levels. MS-64 coins are slightly finer. Some Peace dollars have whitish "milk spots" in the field; while these are not caused by handling, but seem to have been from liquid at the mint or in storage, coins with these spots are rarely graded higher than MS-63 or 64. An MS-65 coin may have minor abrasion, but contact marks are so minute as to require magnification. Luster should be full and rich on earlier issues, and either frosty or satiny on later issues, depending on the date and mint. *Reverse:* At MS-60 some abrasion and contact marks are evident, most noticeably on the eagle's shoulder and nearby. Otherwise, comments apply as for the obverse.

Illustrated coin: Note the scattered marks that are practically definitive of the grade. The high relief of this particular year results in light striking at the center; this is normal and not to be mistaken for wear.

AU-50, 53, 55, 58 (About Uncirculated). *Obverse:* Light wear is seen on the cheek and the highest-relief areas of the hair. The neck truncation edge also shows wear. At AU-58, the luster is extensive, but incomplete. At AU-50 and 53, luster is less but

1934-S. Graded AU-53.

still present. *Reverse:* Wear is evident on the eagle's shoulder and back. Otherwise, comments apply as for the obverse.

Illustrated coin: This coin shows medium and somewhat mottled toning. Luster is still seen in protected areas.

EF-40, 45 (Extremely Fine). *Obverse:* Further wear is seen on the highest-relief areas of the hair, with many strands now blended together. Some luster can usually be seen in protected areas on many coins, but is not needed to define the EF-40 and

1928. Graded EF-40.

45 grades. *Reverse:* Further wear is seen on the eagle, and the upper 60% of the feathers have most detail gone, except for the delineation of the edges of rows of feathers. PEACE shows light wear.

VF-20, 30 (Very Fine). *Obverse:* More wear shows on the hair, with more tiny strands now blended into heavy strands. *Reverse:* Further wear has resulted in very little feather detail except on the neck and tail. The rock shows wear. PEACE is slightly weak.

1934-D. Graded VF-30.

F-12, 15 (Fine). *Obverse:* Most of the hair is worn flat, with thick strands blended together, interrupted by fewer divisions than on higher grades. The rim is full. *Reverse:* Fewer feather details show. Most of the eagle, except for the tail feathers and some

1921. Graded F-12.

traces of feathers at the neck, is in outline only. The rays between the left side of the eagle and PEACE are weak and some details are worn away.

The Peace dollar is seldom collected in grades lower than F-12.

PF-60 to 70 (Proof). *Obverse and Reverse:* Proofs of both types usually display very few handling marks or defects. To qualify as Satin PF-65 or Sandblast PF-65 or finer, contact marks must be microscopic.

1921. Satin Finish Proof.

LIBERTY HEAD DOUBLE EAGLES (1850–1907)

History. The twenty-dollar denomination was introduced to circulation in 1850 (after a unique pattern, which currently resides in the Smithsonian's National Numismatic Collection, was minted in 1849). The large new coin was ideal for converting the flood of California gold rush bullion into federal legal tender. U.S. Mint chief engraver James B. Longacre designed the coin. A different reverse, designed by Anthony Paquet with taller letters than Longacre's design, was tested in 1861 but ultimately not used past that date. In 1866 the motto IN GOD WE TRUST was added to the reverse. In 1877 the denomination on the reverse, formerly given as TWENTY D., was changed to TWENTY DOLLARS. The double eagle denomination proved to be very popular, especially for export. By 1933, more than 75 percent of the American gold used to strike coins from the 1850s onward had been used to make double eagles. Oddly, some of the coins of 1850 to 1858 appear to have the word LIBERTY misspelled as LLBERTY.

Striking and Sharpness. On the obverse, check the star centers and the hair details. As made, the hair details are less distinct on many coins of 1859 (when a slight modification was made) through the 1890s, and knowledge of this is important. Later issues usually have exquisite detail. The reverse usually is well struck, but check the eagle and other features. The denticles are sharp on nearly all coins, but should be checked. Proofs were made in all years from 1858 to 1907, and a few were made before then. Proofs of 1902 onward, particularly 1903, have the portrait polished in the die, imparting a mirror finish across the design, and lack the cameo contrast of earlier dates.

Availability. Basic dates and mintmarks are available in proportion to their mintages. Key issues include the 1854O, 1856-O, 1861 Paquet Reverse, 1861-S Paquet Reverse, 1866 No Motto, 1870-CC, 1879-O, and several Philadelphia Mint dates of the 1880s The vast majority of others are readily collectible. Among early coins, MS examples from about 1854 to 1857 are available, most notably the 1857-S and certain varieties of the 1860s. Most varieties of the 1880s onward, and particularly of the 1890s and 1900s, are easily available in MS, due to the repatriation of millions of coins that had been exported overseas. Proofs dated through the 1870s are all very rare today; those of the 1880s are less so; and those of the 1890s and 1900s are scarce. Many Proofs have been mishandled. Dates that are Proof-only (and those that are very rare in circulation-strike form) are in demand even if impaired. These include 1883, 1884, 1885, 1886, and 1887.

GRADING STANDARDS

MS-60 to 70 (Mint State). *Obverse:* At MS-60, some abrasion and contact marks are evident, most noticeably on the hair to the right of Miss Liberty's forehead and on the cheek. Luster is present, but may be dull or lifeless, and interrupted in patches. At

1876-S. Graded MS-64.

MS-63, contact marks are few, and abrasion is light. An MS-65 coin has little abrasion, and contact marks are minute. Luster should be full and rich. Grades above MS-65 are defined by having fewer marks as perfection is approached. *Reverse:* Comments apply as for the obverse, except that abrasion and contact marks are most noticeable on eagle's neck, wingtips, and tail.

AU-50, 53, 55, 58 (About Uncirculated). *Obverse:* Light wear is seen on the face, the hair to the right of the face, and the highest area of the hair behind the coronet, more so at AU-50 than at 53 or 55. An AU-58 coin has minimal traces of wear. An AU-50

1856-S. Graded AU-53.

coin has luster in protected areas among the stars and letters, with little in the open fields or on the portrait. At AU-58 most luster is present in the fields, but is worn away on the highest parts of the motifs. *Reverse:* Comments as preceding, except that the eagle and ornaments show wear in all of the higher areas. Luster ranges from perhaps 40% remaining in protected areas (at AU-50) to nearly full mint bloom (at AU-58). Often the reverse of this type retains more luster than the obverse.

Illustrated coin: Much of the original luster still remains at this grade level, especially on the reverse.

EF-40, 45 (Extremely Fine). *Obverse:* Wear is evident on all high areas of the portrait, including the hair to the right of the forehead, the tip of the coronet, and hair behind the coronet. The curl to the right of the neck is flat on its highest-relief area.

1855-S. Graded EF-45.

Luster, if present at all, is minimal and in protected areas such as between the star points. *Reverse:* Wear is greater than on an About Uncirculated coin. The eagle's neck and wingtips show wear, as do the ornaments and rays. Some traces of luster may be seen, more so at EF-45 than at EF-40. Overall, the reverse appears to be in a slightly higher grade than the obverse.

VF-20, 30 (Very Fine). *Obverse:* The higher-relief areas of hair are worn flat at VF-20, less so at VF-30. The hair to the right of the coronet is merged into heavy strands and is flat at the back, as is part of the bow. The curl to the

1857-S. Graded VF-20.

right of the neck is flat. *Reverse:* The eagle shows further wear on the head, the tops of the wings, and the tail. The ornament has flat spots.

The Liberty Head double eagle is seldom collected in grades lower than VF-20.

Illustrated coin: Note the small test cut or mark on the top rim.

PF-60 to 70 (Proof). *Obverse and Reverse:* PF-60 to 62 coins have extensive hairlines and may have nicks and contact marks. At PF-63, hairlines are prominent, but the mirror surface is very reflective. PF-64 coins have fewer hairlines. At PF-65, hairlines

1903. Graded PF-64.

should be relatively few. These large and heavy coins reveal hairlines more readily than do the lower denominations, mostly seen only under magnification. PF-66 and higher coins should have no marks or hairlines visible to the unaided eye.

Illustrated coin: A beautiful Proof, this is just a few hairlines away from a higher level.

SAINT-GAUDENS DOUBLE EAGLES (1907–1933)

History. In autumn 1907 U.S. Mint chief engraver Charles E. Barber modified Augustus Saint-Gaudens's design by lowering its relief and substituting Arabic (not Roman) numerals. Coins of this type were struck in large quantities from 1907 to 1916 and again from 1920 to 1933. In July 1908 the motto IN GOD WE TRUST was added to the reverse. Coins dated 1907 to 1911 have 46 stars on the obverse; coins of 1912 to 1933 have 48 stars. Sandblast (also called Matte) Proofs were made in 1908 and from 1911 to 1915; Satin (also called Roman Finish) Proofs were made in 1909 and 1910.

The vast majority of these coins were exported. Since World War II millions have been repatriated, supplying most of those in numismatic hands today.

Striking and Sharpness. The details are often light on the obverse. Check the bosom of Miss Liberty, the covering of which tends to be weak on 1907 and, especially, 1908 No Motto coins. Check the Capitol building and its immediate area at the lower left. The reverse usually is well struck, but check the feathers on the eagle and the top of the wings. The Matte

Proofs have dull surfaces, much like finegrained sandpaper, while the Satin Proofs have satiny surfaces and are bright yellow.

Availability. Most dates and mintmarks range from very common to slightly scarce, punctuated with scarce to very rare issues such as 1908-S, 1920-S, 1921, mintmarked coins from 1924 to 1927, and all issues of 1929 to 1933. From their initial mintages, most of the double eagles of the 1920s were returned to the Mint and melted in the 1930s. Some, however, were unofficially saved by Treasury employees. Estimates of the quantities saved range from a few dozen to several hundred thousand, depending on the date; this explains the high values for coins that, judged only by their initial mintages, should otherwise be more common. Probably a million or more MS coins exist of certain dates, most notably 1908 No Motto, 1924, 1925, 1926, and 1928 (especially common). Quality varies, as many have contact marks. Philadelphia Mint coins from 1922 onward usually are seen with excellent eye appeal. Common varieties are not usually collected in grades below MS. All of the Proofs are rare today.

GRADING STANDARDS

MS-60 to 70 (Mint State). *Obverse:* At MS-60, some abrasion and contact marks are seen on Liberty's chest and left knee, and scattered marks and abrasion are in the field. Luster is present, but may be dull or lifeless, and interrupted in patches. At MS-63, con-

1924. Graded MS-65.

tact marks are fewer, and abrasion is light. An MS-65 coin has little abrasion and few marks, although quality among certified coins can vary. On a conservatively graded coin the luster should be full and rich. Grades above MS-65 are defined by having fewer marks as perfection is approached. Generally, Mint State coins of 1922 onward are choicer and more attractive than the earlier issues. *Reverse:* Comments apply as for the obverse, except that abrasion and contact marks are most noticeable on the eagle's left wing.

AU-50, 53, 55, 58 (About Uncirculated). *Obverse:* Light wear is seen on the chest, the left knee, the midriff, and across the field, more so at AU-50 than at 53 or 55. An AU-58 coin has minimal traces of wear. An AU-50 coin has luster in protected areas among the rays, with little in the open field above. At AU-58, most luster is present. *Reverse:* Comments as preceding, except that the side of the eagle below the front of the wing, the top of the wing, and the field show light wear. Luster ranges from 40% (at AU-50) to nearly full mint bloom (at AU-58).

1909, 9 Over 8. Graded AU-50.

EF-40, 45 (Extremely Fine). *Obverse:* Wear is seen on all the higher-relief areas of the standing figure and on the rock at the lower right. Luster is minimal, if present at all. Eye appeal is apt to be lacking. *Reverse:* The eagle shows more wear overall, especially at the bottom and on the tops of the wings.

1908-S. Graded EF-40.

VF-20, 30 (Very Fine). *Obverse:* Most details of the standing figure are flat, her face is incomplete, and the tips of the rays are weak. Eye appeal is usually poor. *Reverse:* Wear is greater overall, but most evident on the eagle. Detail is good at the center of the left wing, but worn away in most other areas of the bird.

1914. Graded VF-20.

PF-60 to 70 (Proof). *Obverse and Reverse:* At PF-60 to 63, there is light abrasion and some contact marks. On Sandblast Proofs these show up as visually unappealing bright spots. At PF-64 and higher levels, marks are fewer, with magnification needed to see any at PF-65. At PF-66, there should be none at all.

1909, Satin Finish. Graded PF-66.

APPENDIX B

Coin-Collecting Resources

The following resources may be of value to you in your efforts to learn more about coin collecting and to find venues for buying and selling. Note that this is an abbreviated list and far from complete; many other worthwhile resources exist.

Coin Certification

ANACS, www.anacs.com
Independent Coin Graders (ICG), www.icgcoin.com
Numismatic Guaranty Corporation (NGC), www.ngccoin.com
Professional Coin Grading Service (PCGS), www.pcgs.com
SEGS Inc., www.segsgrading.com

Government Mints and Institutions

Banco de México (Bank of Mexico), www.banxico.org.mx/indexEn.html
British Royal Mint, www.royalmint.com
Bureau of Engraving and Printing, www.bep.treas.gov
Central Mint (of China), www.cmc.gov.tw/
Monnaie de Paris (Paris Mint), www.monnaiedeparis.com
National Numismatic Collection, Smithsonian,
    americanhistory.si.edu/collections/object-groups/
    national-numismatic-collection
Royal Australian Mint, www.ramint.gov.au
Royal Canadian Mint, www.mint.ca
San Francisco Federal Reserve Bank, www.frbsf.org
South African Mint Company, www.samint.co.za
United States Mint, www.usmint.gov

Numismatic Education: Books

The Coin Collector's Survival Manual, by Scott Travers
    (House of Collectibles)
Official ANA Grading Standards Guide for United States Coins, by Kenneth
    Bressett (Whitman Publishing)
A Guide to United States Coins (the "Red Book"), by R.S. Yeoman
    (Whitman Publishing)

Numismatic Education: Web Sites

American Numismatic Association (ANA), www.money.org
American Numismatic Society, www.numismatics.org
Coin & Currency Institute, www.coin-currency.com

Numismatic Education: Specialty Clubs

Barber Coin Collectors' Society, www.barbercoins.org
Early American Coppers, www.eacs.org
Fly-In Club, fly-inclub.org
John Reich Collectors Society, logan.com/jrcs
Liberty Seated Collectors Club, www.lsccweb.org
Lincoln Cent Forum, www.lincolncentforum.com
Shield Nickels, groups.yahoo.com/group/Shield_Nickels
Society of Paper Money Collectors, www.spmc.org

Numismatic Publishers

Amos Press (publishers of *Coin World*), www.coinworld.com
Krause Publications, www.krause.com
Miller Magazines (publishers of *CoinAge*), www.coinagemag.com
Whitman Publishing, www.whitman.com

Numismatic Software

Carlisle Development Corporation, www.carlisledevelopment.com
Trove Software, www.trovesoftware.com

Sales Venues: Major Auction Houses

Classical Numismatic Group, Inc. (specializing in classical, medieval, and
    British coins), www.cngcoins.com
Heritage Auctions, www.ha.com
Stack's Bowers Galleries, www.stacksbowers.com
Lyn Knight Currency Auctions (specializing in U.S. and world paper money),
    www.lynknight.com
Ira & Larry Goldberg Auctioneers, www.goldbergcoins.com

Sales Venues: Online Auctions

Teletrade, www.teletrade.com
eBay, www.ebay.com
Holabird-Kagin Americana, www.holabirdamericana.com
GreatCollections, www.greatcollections.com

Sales Venues: Precious Metal Refiners

Garfield Refining, www.garfieldrefining.com

Sales Venues: Dealer-Related Sites

International Association of Professional Numismatists (IAPN),
    www.iapn-coins.org
Professional Numismatists Guild (PNG), www.pngdealers.com

Acknowledgements & About the Author

This book is the result of many conversations with collectors who have used the coin-collecting software products published by Carlisle Development Corporation. Most users are either in retirement or nearing retirement and are grappling with the decisions as to what to do with regards to their coin collecting interest.

I have learned much from these conversations, and in particular have discerned some common threads. These in turn have encouraged me to author this work, which is intended to share what I have learned.

I'd also like to acknowledge my family members, who have supported my efforts and without whom Carlisle Development Corporation would not exist.

Tom Bilotta developed an interest in numismatics during his childhood. His new passion was encouraged by his father, Domenic, a life-long collector. Tom earned both bachelor's and master's degrees in electrical engineering from Massachusetts Institute of Technology in 1973 and went on to serve in a variety of engineering, management, and executive positions involving software development for a variety of applications and operating systems.

In 1994 Tom, with the support of his wife Marie, founded Carlisle Development Corporation, today a leading publisher of numismatic software. This new venture allowed him to bring together his interests in numismatics and software and has since produced a comprehensive product line of numismatic inventory and educational software programs. Over the years, Carlisle Development and its products have received a number of awards from the Numismatic Literary Guild and also from publications such as *PC Magazine.*

As a result of his work at Carlisle Development, Tom has interacted with countless numismatists, many of whom are retired or are approaching retirement. He has also spoken to many heirs who have inherited a coin collection without any guidance as to how to manage its continuation or liquidation. These conversations ultimately resulted in the material presented in this book.

Glossary

Over the years coin collectors have developed a special jargon to describe their coins. The following list includes terms that are used frequently by coin collectors or that have a special meaning other than their ordinary dictionary definitions. You will find them useful when you want to discuss or describe your coins.

alloy—A combination of two or more metals.

bronze—An alloy of copper, zinc, and tin.

bullion—Uncoined gold or silver in the form of bars, ingots, or plate.

cent—One one-hundredth of the standard monetary unit. Also known as a centavo, centimo, or centesimo in some Central American and South American countries; centime in France and various former colonies in Africa; and other variations.

certified coin—A coin that has been graded, authenticated, and encapsulated in plastic by an independent (neither buyer nor seller) grading service.

cherrypicker—A collector who finds scarce and unusual coins by carefully searching through unattributed items in old accumulations or dealers' stocks.

circulation strike—An Uncirculated coin intended for eventual use in commerce, as opposed to a Proof coin.

contact marks—Minor abrasions on an Uncirculated coin, made by contact with other coins in a bag or roll.

die—A piece of metal engraved with a design and used for stamping coins.

die variety—Any minor alteration in the basic design of a coin.

dipped, dipping—Refers to chemical cleaning of a coin to remove oxidation or foreign matter.

double eagle—The United States twenty-dollar gold coin.

doubled die—A die that has been given two misaligned impressions from a hub; also, a coin made from such a die.

eagle—A United States ten-dollar gold coin; also refers to U.S. silver, gold, and platinum bullion pieces made from 1986 to the present.

edge—Periphery of a coin, often with reeding, lettering, or other decoration.

encapsulated coins—Coins that have been authenticated, graded, and sealed in plastic by a professional service.

error—A mismade coin not intended for circulation.

field—The background portion of a coin's surface not used for a design or inscription.

filler—A coin in worn condition but rare enough to be included in a collection.

fineness—The purity of gold, silver, or any other precious metal, expressed in terms of one thousand parts. A coin of 90% pure silver is expressed as .900 fine.

gem—A coin of exceptionally high quality, typically considered MS-65 or PF-65 or better.

grade risk—The financial risk a purchaser takes on when buying an uncertified coin at the price point of its assumed or estimated grade. Should that coin actually be of a lower grade than that originally estimated, the purchaser would not be able to recoup their initial investment.

half eagle—The United States five-dollar gold coin minted from 1795 to 1929.

hub—A positive-image punch to impress the coin's design into a die for coinage.

intrinsic value—Bullion or "melt" value of the actual precious metal in a numismatic item.

investment grade—Promotional term; generally, a coin in grade MS-65 or better.

junk silver—Common-date silver coins taken from circulation; worth only bullion value.

key coin (or key date)—One of the scarcer or more valuable coins in a series.

legal tender—Money that is officially issued and recognized for redemption by an authorized agency or government.

luster—The brilliant or "frosty" surface quality of an Uncirculated (Mint State) coin.

mintmark—A small letter or other mark on a coin, indicating the mint at which it was struck.

Mint set—A set of Uncirculated coins packaged and sold by the Mint. Each set contains one of each of the coins made for circulation at each of the mints that year.

obverse—The front or face side of a coin.

overdate—Date made by superimposing one or more numerals on a previously dated die.

overgraded—A coin in poorer condition than stated.

pattern—Experimental or trial coin, generally of a new design, denomination, or metal.

PayPal—An electronic commerce (e-commerce) company that facilitates payments between parties through online funds transfers.

Proof—Coins struck for collectors by the Mint using specially polished dies and planchets.

Proof set—A set of each of the Proof coins made during a given year, packaged by the Mint and sold to collectors.

quarter eagle—The United States $2.50 gold coin.

raw—A coin that has not been encapsulated by an independent grading service.

reserve—a minimum dollar amount that the owner of an item up for auction will accept as the winning bid in the auction.

reverse—The back side of a coin.

rim—The raised portion of a coin that protects the design from wear.

series—A set of one coin of each year of a specific design and denomination issued from each mint. For example, Lincoln cents from 1909 to 1959.

slab—A hard plastic case containing a coin that has been graded and encapsulated by a professional service.

spot price—The daily quoted market value of precious metals in bullion form.

token—A privately issued piece, typically with an exchange value for goods or services, but not an official government coin.

type—A series of coins defined by a shared distinguishing design, composition, denomination, and other elements. For example, Barber dimes or Franklin half dollars.

type set—A collection consisting of one representative coin of each type, of a particular series or period.

Uncirculated—A circulation-strike coin that has never been used in commerce, and has retained its original surface and luster; also called Mint State.

variety—A coin's design that sets it apart from the normal issue of that type.

year set—A set of coins for any given year, consisting of one of each denomination issued that year.

Index

allocation methods 81–101

altered coins
    colorized 23
    elongated 120, 121

ANACS (formerly the certification service of the American Numismatic Association) 47, 64, 65, 127

bags (of coins).. 17, 20–23

Cash in Your Coins: Selling the Rare Coins You've Inherited 106, 107

certification 43, 47, 49, 52, 62–67, 99, 116–118, 122, 123, 129, 153–159, 165

Certified Acceptance Corporation 155, 156

cleaning (of coins).. 71, 73

coin albums 10–14

coin shows 41, 131

colonial coins 39, 121

commemorative coins........................ 162–164, 166, 167

eBay (and sales of coins via eBay) 51, 52, 135, 161–171

estate taxes..145–147

Expert's Guide to Collecting and Investing in Rare Coins, The 115

die varieties and error coins............................... 57, 118

foreign coins.......................28, 29, 34, 35, 39, 40, 60, 61

gifting coins........................55, 87, 88, 94, 139, 140, 147

grade risk... 43, 49

Guide Book of United States Coins (the "Red Book") ... 21, 27, 38, 39, 53, 91, 106, 130

Handbook of United States Coins (the "Blue Book") 53, 132

hobo nickels 119

Independent Coin Graders (ICG)..................... 65, 127

insurance (for a collection) 74

inventory.............19, 24, 25, 97, 105, 106, 110, 111, 116
    software 24, 25, 104, 105

Kennedy World in Medallic Art, The............................. 168

key date.. 22

liquidation (of a collection; see also sales methods) . 6, 9, 14, 18, 21, 31, 43, 44, 137, 138

medals... 119

Mint sets.................................12, 17, 20, 21, 56, 57, 127

Numismatic Guaranty Corporation (NGC) .. 47, 64, 65, 69, 117, 127, 158

numismatic publications 10, 45
    Coin Dealer Newsletter (and the "Greysheet") ... 27, 47, 50–53, 69, 99, 132
    Coin World (and *Coin World Values*) 47, 53, 55, 69, 99
    Numismatic News.. 55

pattern coins 119

PayPal 170, 171

placing coins back in circulation..................... 140, 141

plated coins 60

Professional Coin Grading Service (PCGS) .. 47, 64, 65, 69, 117, 127, 158

Professional Numismatists Guild 69

Proof sets 12, 17, 20, 21, 56, 57, 127

registry sets 158, 159

rolls (of coins).. 17, 20–23

sales methods 26, 31, 45, 46, 62, 90, 91, 97, 110–112, 125–127, 129
    auction (in-person) 134, 135
    auction (online; see also eBay) ... 14, 45, 51, 52, 112, 134, 135
    bulk (and mail-order) 14, 19, 22, 50, 55, 112, 126, 127, 132, 139
    consignment 14, 45, 47–49, 130–132
    local dealer 14, 43, 47, 49, 110, 111, 130–134

security (of your collection)..................................73–75

selling for bullion value................................ 58–60, 159

"slabs" (plastic holders used by certification companies; see also certification)..................... 12, 62

special designations (appended to coin grades)....153–155

storage (of coins) 71, 159
    polyvinyl chloride (PVC) flips......................... 71, 72

technology (and use in relation to numismatics) 7, 175–191,

thematic collections.............................. 34–41, 149, 150

tokens.. 119
    Civil War.. 34
    Hard Times.. 38
    transportation.. 38

tubes (of coins) 20–22

turning coins into the bank 21, 24, 139